AN INSIGNIFICANT LIFE

AN INSIGNIFICANT LIFE

✦

Overcoming the Fear of Being Gay

BOOK FOUR

Miracle T. Kelly

iUniverse, Inc.

New York Lincoln Shanghai

AN INSIGNIFICANT LIFE
Overcoming the Fear of Being Gay

iUniverse books may be ordered through booksellers or by contacting:

iUniverse
2021 Pine Lake Road, Suite 100
Lincoln, NE 68512
www.iuniverse.com
1-800-Authors (1-800-288-4677)

The views expressed in this work are solely those of the author and do not necessarily reflect the views of the publisher, and the publisher hereby disclaims any responsibility for them.

ISBN-13: 978-0-595-42065-0 (pbk)
ISBN-13: 978-0-595-86410-2 (ebk)
ISBN-10: 0-595-42065-6 (pbk)
ISBN-10: 0-595-86410-4 (ebk)

Printed in the United States of America

This book is dedicated to the youth in society whom struggle with the knowledge of being gay and how to share this with your parents, siblings and friends. Be the best person you can, communicate, educate and never stop loving your family even if they can't accept who you truly are. Have faith in your God whichever denomination you are all else shall work out in His time.

I've always thought of myself as an irregular girl. Contrary to appearances I am not of the conforming nature of the female species inside or out. Therefore, I am living proof that one cannot judge a book by its cover. In essence we all have our own personal story to tell and truth be known, I may be described as a walking controversy.

Contents

CONTEMPLATION

I knew this day would come but I thought surely I would be better prepared. At what point do you stop being, feeling responsible for your family and begin taking care of yourself? Strong family traditions and obligations are deeply rooted within me. My duty to God most of all about being the best person I can and do for others long before I did for myself is at the center of my anguish and turmoil. My apprehension about sharing my true identity has always been a matter between my Father and me first before my parents, siblings and friends. Yet how do I separate or limit such discipline without self-destructing because the individual is suffering?

There is nothing more sad or incomprehensible then a life of loneliness. Where does loyalty to one's self start and family end without loss of respect? I am at the point in my life where my very existence is a tapestry of contemplation. I have graduated high school and now am thrust upon a future without any direction or plan of what to do next. I am in a perpetual state of abject misery. I realize that I am not a grounded soul and have no expectations of self. I have obligations and commitments to others bound by strong family traditions and religious beliefs. I do not care about what happens to me and care even less how I exist.

I'm currently engaged in a sexual affair with a married man with children and every time he indulges in me I am not there in either spirit or mind. I felt nothing as well as made no attempts to share any excitement with what was happening. Sexual relations with men are unnatural acts of aggression and hostile role playing against myself for being so weak. In acting the typical female of being readily available for sexual encounters is a dark side of myself I could neither fight nor contain. I submerged deep down into the dungeon of my soul once again where I could safely hide.

These encounters only compounded the hate and anger toward myself which grew deeper with each experience. I lay there as limp as a dead bird in the tight clutches of its captor, the stalky neighborhood cat, no emotions and very much unresponsive. I had accomplished none of my hopes or dreams and therefore felt even more worthless. I look back at my insignificant life and grieve for the two most significant people whom died when I was much younger. I've never been able to regain my composure since their deaths. Both of them especially traumatic for me personally and I hid that well from all others. Since then I have been totally and absolutely alone, never have I felt as empty as I do now.

Not even God would bother with me now. I adopted early on the fatalistic attitude that every day was a good day to die and I secretly wished; prayed for that with every waking moment being my last. I did not want to go any further or on any longer struggling to have any sort of relationship whether it's my family or another humane being. I could not see past the early morning dawn where everything is so peaceful and quiet, nothing but the songbirds outside my window serenading the rising sun. For as long as I could remember when I was able to think for myself, three years old to be exact, I knew there was a change occurring that I could not prevent or stop it's direction. My transition into oblivion was not only immediate but profound. There seems no closure for people like me with a shameful past.

I had plunged into my own reality face to face finally in the moment I stepped on the Greyhound bus heading back to Glendale. My life in Oceanside has concluded and now I must decide what to do next. I left willingly and didn't look back for one instant as I was keenly aware that my use to family and friends was no more. It had become clear to me on that long ride back that things at home had definitely changed. I had lost my position in the pecking order at home and was no longer a necessity. They all had grown accustomed to my absence and anything I said or did really didn't matter anymore. In their eyes, I too had moved on. I was a week-end visitor, an older sibling whose only duty now is being responsible for sending money home to help support the family. Mother never asked this of me yet it was more an understanding. The older sibling's right of passage is family duty.

My energy slowly depleting, I have no reason to think there is any future for me. I unconsciously hurt or drove away those who cared or tried to love me. I simply did not know how to deal with others who showed concern for me or often if truth be known, I misinterpreted their empathy for something else. I didn't know what love was or what it meant. I admit that I am a complex individual and know if I'm going to have any semblance of a life beyond this, I need therapy. Perhaps on one of my visits back home this summer I may join the family in a visit with their therapist. Trust is a resource I have very little of but I must try I know.

I am truly on my own, dependent on my own self-sufficiency. I have been trapped inside myself for so long I don't know how to conduct an ordinary life. What behaviors are most appropriate when what drives me from within is to be natural, to be queer? My desires, emotionally and physically for companionship is mirror image to myself. I crave the silence like an addiction and feed off the quiet of night. This is when I am truly alive and most creative. My passions in life have always included the little people because of their compelling ability to be truthful and honest about how they perceive life and everything around them. Their environment is much different then how adults judge it. Children are unaware of sin until something unordinary happens to them. They learn what they are taught and live by the experiences of daily life. Children know no wrong until they are introduced. They know no ill feelings until they are shown. My life in the beginning was filled with a child's excitement and thirst wanting to know things, all things.

I could relate to the dreams children share with me and the unexpected stories they tell just about everything! I am fascinated by their innocence and hopeful that they will grow up unabashed as I had been at their age. As deeply rooted as my faith in God is, I am uncertain of which direction to go at this point in my life. I am on my own and making money but I have no idea what to do now! Animals have always been a source of comfort and companionship for me when life was being cruel. They seemed to keep me centered and their love always unconditional. I could find hope in myself whenever I was with a family pet and their presence encouraged me.

Yet there is a fire that smolders in my soul and often leaves layers of heavy soot for me to walk through. I look back at these footprints with trepidation and curiosity. Sometimes they are the size of a small child and others like my own, youthful wavering on adulthood. Relationships are cautiously maneuvered around as I try to accommodate my partner in whatever pleases him while my own wants and needs are unimportant. I seem to always love the things that matter least to others; like the twirling of leaves which desperately hold on to the branches where they reside on a windy day. I can image myself as those very leaves fighting to stay attached and not ripped away by the force of Mother Nature.

I love watching the clouds dancing with one another passing overhead against the light blue sky. Remembering how Matthew and I would lay upon the grass in the backyard for hours trying to make out their shapes and the soft feel of the unmowed grass which I felt sustained my bodyweight as if they were a million tiny pillars. There is a life untouched within me protected by the hand of God which covets the loss I suffered as a child. That place I went to, my spirit and soul wounded by a familiar person who indulged himself in the pleasures of a small child. I understood at a very young age while learning about God and all His creation that of all God's creations, children are His greatest glory. As much as there should be comfort in this knowledge, I've come to know likewise.

My search for a God whom I had learned so much about from Grandmother and family praying was nowhere to be found in those first moments of horror! I am still terrorized by those memories anytime I see him even though I have baby-sat his children on dozens of occasions. I could not let him know that he affected me this way or else it would open the door for him to pursue me once again. I would still be unable to escape as every time I was around him I felt paralyzed as if I had become that three year old little girl once again believing and trusting in him that we were simply going to lay down for a nap. Children know nothing about the contexts of sex and they never should!

I felt like an orphan left in the cold at the steps of a church with its heavy wide doors unopened with a fast approaching storm filled with violence and uncertainty. I was not afraid because I didn't know how to be. I had lost much of any fear I possessed after the last incident when I walked off with that stranger on one of my many trips to town with Kammillie. To this day I cannot stand the feel of chiffon upon my skin and reflected back to those moments when that stranger loosely wrapped that pink chiffon scarf around my neck asking me "did I like it"? In that instant, staring into his eyes, I knew he was going to kill me and I was prepared to die without a doubt in my mind.

I am not afraid of death like other people are but instead I welcome it with an open mind and heart. If anything is for certain in one's life, death is something none of us can escape. I spent a childhood looking for God, praying for a sign and no matter how embedded my faith is, hope was lost so many years ago. I thought I found a love that I could understand or at least grow to relate to being as we were of similar natures. However there were circumstances beyond my control that drove him elsewhere and I was abandoned. That single failure after sacrificing so much, after betraying my own self, had plummeted me into a state of depression that I still have not completely recovered.

As easy as it is to mask and pretend that everything is alright, I suffer an exhaustive sense of humiliation. I return to the memories of my childhood just so I don't have to think about what to do. I remember as a child I would see creatures with the most delicate wings such as the dragonfly or butterfly as angels in training. The fluttering of butterflies upon the soft belly of daisies brought such joy to my face and heart. I was amazed that their sheer wings looked as though they would disintegrate if you touched them. I remember fondly my first introduction to them just as they emerged from their cocoon which I always found hanging underneath the wooden fence post.

I thought about all those times when the ocean spit me out onto the shore as a child growing up who braved the mysterious and unpredictable cycle of waves. Even though I could not swim very well at that age, I loved the challenge and how it called to me to go further out and test my will. I knew there were people on guard watching and God was somewhere high above observing as well. I knew that if ever I was in trouble He would send his angels to rescue me and extract me from this playful sea. I loved the ocean for some reason, the vastness of it all and how the pelicans barely skimmed the tops of the water as they flew by in pairs or small groups.

I am cognizant that there are different versions of myself and that I must nurture each of them accordingly no matter how complex it may seem to get. I discovered these at a very young age but didn't know what to do because there was nobody to talk to and I was always afraid that if I shared this information with the wrong people mom would send me to some institution! It's not a matter of hearing voices or becoming different personalities or even that I was a boy trapped inside this girls body. It's what the American Indians refer to as two spirits, possessing both male and female spirits.

I am at an intersection of my life in which whatever choice I make has got to be the right choice. There are so many things to consider that only I can determine there priority. Completing high school, having been employed since my birthday in January and establishing a small savings account while divvying up the rest to family and my place of residence should speak to my level of maturity but it doesn't. Clearly now that reality sets in, I'm out of school, living away from home there are definite decisions I must deal with. The real me, the strong, assertive, passionate and empathetic person I know me to be is ready and willing to take the next step and confront mom and the family about myself.

Yet that child which resides in the dungeon of my soul has the most unbelievable power over my true identity that I am reduced to being ultra passive and weak in the worst possible way. My inner turmoil I fear is going to lead me to an early death. Writing has been my passion since I learned to put words in a sentence and was given an assignment to write the story of what I did this summer. I keep diaries, journals and pads of paper everywhere I go. As a writer you can tell the story however you like and the reader knows no difference. My desire is to write the truth and as painful as I know it will be to me, it is a necessary evil.

Inescapable this place called depression. A well so deep I fear that once I hit bottom there will be no way out. I have only one drop of hope left and I fear I'm losing my grip on that! I cannot restrain my journey inward for I am obsessed, consumed with the thought of dying. I've lived a life I want no part of nor care to participate in any longer. I move invisibly in and out of my reality knowing that, which I am, a woman who desires the companionship of another woman but is not what I am, that desire does not define me. I find solace in the silence of the night as though I was a nocturnal creature.

It is my refuge and the glimmering stars afford me enough light to be as I am. I live my life in shades of black and red. In these colors, black represents my friend and foe the darkness, contentment, solitude and refuge from the light. Red represents shame, deep seeded anger at almost every living adult who has picked away a part of my life like a vulture eats a corpse with no regard of it's after affects. I've gone through life feeling nothing, so therefore I am nothing; I fear nothing and no one not even death itself. Something I yearn for on a daily basis with every waking moment like a newborn after their mother's breast for food.

I seek death as the only solution to my lifelong anguish and torment. Having to deal with my moody unpredictable character is what's most disturbing for me. I cannot bear to think that I have a mental disorder and won't accept that conclusion. How long must I live in purgatory? I feel I have failed my siblings in that I was unable to keep my composure after the break-up with Mark. My dramatic weight loss was in protest of failing the simplest of tests; conducting a simple and loving relationship with another person. It was beside the point; that our relationship was a farce but none the less. I gave everything humanely possibly in every way, shape and form; unconditional love, freedom and every chance to become a parent.

No longer am I my sisters mentor for in my absence I have lost face. What to do next because I have always been the care taker in our family since I was little and my sisters were babies. It's what I learned to live for after the first assault. I need to think about my life now without feeling guilty for leaving my family. But how do I do that? Granted life has always been difficult, filled with anguish and tormented not just by childhood experiences but at other choices I've made as well. Hiding the truth is the heaviest burden I carry. In spite of my fierce independence and self sufficient character there is a deep need within me to care for others.

I need to be needed in order to go on, it's what motivates and inspires me. So much of me is driven by what and how I can assist others. A part of me strongly desires to join the Marine Corps and get an education in a field I know will have a lasting career outside the military. Law enforcement has always held an interest for me because a lot of what they do is helping others in one way or another. Perhaps studying to be a detective or working with juveniles which is what interests me most of all. Yet wanting to do this and actually signing the papers with a recruiter is a whole other story.

I've always done well with children and youth because it's so easy for me to relate to their issues, their anger and lack of discipline. Who do they have to mentor them if it's not their parents, siblings or teachers? My insatiable need to help others can be blinding for the bigger picture here. I do not see myself spending my life doing factory work! As a child, teachers were my mentors and hero's so perhaps I should take that avenue. I also love to read and write perhaps I could be a writer as well which in a way is a form of teaching. There are plenty of options I know to choose from but I lack support which is always essential for low esteem people like me.

Life is filled with obstacles and thus far have I managed to get around most of them with minimal setback. Then there are the deeper issues I need to address that are emotional walls for me but I have yet to meet anyone I feel I can trust. I've always been seen as a strong one in the family emotionally but that couldn't be further from the truth. I have people in my life I trust with my life but to expose my true identity is a risk I'm not willing to take, they are all I truly have. Mrs. Kaahaaina has been my surrogate mother since sixth grade, cousin Cecilia is more my sister then cousin and Mrs. Moore, my softball coach is a woman I respect and love deeply.

There are pieces of thread which are all there is holding my quilted life together. I feel remorse and shame for destroying the friendships of two other very special people in my life. It was at a time of great darkness for me that I had become lost and misjudged their kindness. In my heart I fell in love with a teacher of mine from junior high school that shattered my heart and have not even to this day recovered from that catastrophe. I believe there should be a course in school that deals with adolescent emotions in which the instructor could prepare the student for what may come. To expose the students the variety of feelings and how to behave and conduct one's self appropriately.

I can assure you it was not adolescent infatuation of an older woman. I could not sleep at night, concentrate on my studies, eat regularly or think of anything but her! Boys were a distraction but whenever I kissed one of them I was truly kissing her! I am working hard to keep my reality of all my difficulties locked up in the deepest corner of my soul. Living has suddenly become harder because I am not afraid of dying. I am a student of self-destructive behavior. I do not subscribe to the opinions of others whom condemn my true identity of being gay including my mother.

There are the suppositions of for instance; *are you sure it's not just a phase? Do you want to have a sex change? Do you feel like a boy trapped inside a girls body* is perhaps the most frequent question. I should be offended or at the least embarrassed for them but I realize it is their lack of education that brings them to such a state of ignorance. I have an inquiring interest myself along those same lines. I stop for just a brief moment to ponder these three questions and direct them at myself. I know for certain the first question is a definite absolutely not! However the later two need a little longer thought processing.

However their observations are not entirely without merit. As a closeted lesbian, which by the way I despise labels, I can see how they would come to this conclusion. There is a woman at work whom countless others have warned me about because of *"what she is"*. I do not allow others to pick and choose my friends and acquaintances for me. That is one freedom I refuse to relinquish for anybody. If anything it will push me closer to them for I have always been drawn to those who are ridiculed and gossiped about. I have never thought myself to be better then anyone else. This I learned from my dad and Grandmother.

Therapy may be the only alternative there is which can set me free. Naturally I will have my own series of test for her to see if I can trust her. My expectations are limited depending on how our initial meeting goes. As with anything, the results will depend upon how willing I am to share. My biggest want is learning how to deal with the inner conflict between the child within; Terry and myself, my true identity. It will be my only agenda to reveal this identity, share my torment about who I am, have always been as opposed to what I appear to be as an ordinary girl.

My strong willingness to do this is not without some apprehension in that my biggest fear is I will be mistaken of or misdiagnosed as having dual personalities. I am not my mother's daughter and therefore I cannot be prejudged by the history of family disorders. I refuse to be classified as having a fixable condition. Doubt is my own worst enemy and I know I cannot let this defeat me now. I'm eighteen and dying to get out of this hell I live within. Loneliness is the one power I have always succumbed to and fear the most. My splintered relationship with God sustains me in the depths of my despair but is in need of serious repair.

I have never doubted His presence somewhere in my life but I also am aware that suicide is a forgivable sin. I am already dead so what real difference would it make to take a life which is without purpose? I cannot control my anger so I drink to ease the pain. I have gained more weight by this unhealthy behavior which in turn creates a monster in itself. I have ended the relationship with this man and in the interim become friendly with a kind stranger closer to my age. I have become totally oblivious to the wants and needs of myself and set aside the goals I jotted down on my trip back here.

I find hard alcohol repulsive but continue to drink heavily, Jack Daniels whiskey the choice of consumption. My relatives have not brought to my attention the unhealthy behavior I've exhibited lately and perhaps they may think it's just a transitional thing. I spend as much time with them as possible on week-ends. Richard and Betty have three wonderful, energetic children; Richard Jr., Anthony and Lacy. My cousins Eddie and Cecilia live just a few doors up the street and are in fact neighbors while my Uncle Felix and Aunt Connie further up the same street. They all have three children as well, how ironic!

I have taken care of each of the families with the exception of Eddies because his wife Mary doesn't work. But Cecilia, her children; Mike, Gabriella and Danny I have the most experience with. I have stayed with them while I was in school in the past, spending some summer weeks here. I have a deep sense of closeness with Cecilia because she means something special to me. She's like mom in a sense with having a temper but she works just as hard and loves her children with everything she has. I have always felt closeness towards her because she is a model individual regardless.

We have always had fun on junking trips through the back streets and alleys of Beverly Hills and other exclusive neighborhoods in our younger years before all the kids came. Nobody ever questioned me when I was out late but did return back home before curfew even if I did forget to call once or twice. One evening I took a trip to an unknown destination with this guy I had met some weeks before and I had no reservations about where we were headed either. I never though anything bad or evil would happen to me that hadn't already occurred! We ended up at a reservoir or some large body of water behind a wall.

Pitch dark and not many stars in the sky. You could barley see the city lights off in the distance and we began to talk in a low tone. We listened mostly to the creatures whose environment we had invaded. There were the crickets and bullfrogs and other four legged inhabitants of the landscape whom we could not see but heard clearly. We drank just a little sloe gin and talked briefly about what my plans might be now that I'm out of school. He wanted to be a police officer; I said I was undecided at the moment. It was a lame response but it was the truth.

We continued our evening engaging in an unsuccessful sexual encounter because neither one of us for some reason could not commit to the process in which we were involved. I was not completed afraid of the handcuff incident but I figured if this was something he would need to have me engaged in for to long a period I would certainly miss my curfew and be prohibited from seeing him for an unknown period of time. With that revelation he slowly unlocked the cuffs and we returned to the car where we headed back to town. He seemed a descent guy, quiet but kind and I had no reason to fear otherwise.

Work was going alright and I wasn't in any hurry to go home anytime soon. All the cousins packed up their cars one Saturday for a trip to Knott's Berry Farm. Family outings always brought me back down to earth. I am deeply family oriented and it pains me I am seemingly estranged from my own. I ended the courtship with my friend all for the better I felt. I was still being somewhat pursued by my former acquaintance which I continue to make excuses to put him off. The guilt is overwhelming and so I do whatever is necessary to ignore his calls or dole out reason's why I cannot make it that evening.

On week-ends I still drink more then I should but I sneak the liquor so they don't think I've had too much, after all I am still a minor. With July fourth fast approaching I haven't decided one way or the other about going home for the long week-end. I prefer to stay here but we'll have to wait and see. Home always made me uneasy and it was bad enough that I was already on a very dangerous and unpredictable road of self-destruction. I knew I could not go much further with the scandalous affair I was in and out of. The entire concept of any degree of sexual contact with a male was unnatural for me. I always gave in because it was expected and I have been completely destroyed as a humane being.

The struggle just doesn't seem important enough. More times then not I have failed at my attempts to overcome my inadequacies. I try very hard to be a better person and to do the right things by family and friends with the end result disappointing. Those who were most influential in my life have passed away or moved on. I am weary to make new friends because people always seem to have ulterior motives. I want my friends to be as sincere and true to heart as I am. Surrounding myself with good, positive and loving people can only bring out those emotions in me.

I have often expressed my passions in life being close with the little people of the world because of their compelling truths and dreams that they are so free and willing to share. Also my love and respect for the animals because they bring me the greatest sense of comfort and loyalty without expecting any less in return. All my life we have been raised with all sorts of animals and often a variety at the same time. They bring me comfort and know just how to keep me centered. I think often that I am here by mistake, that my birth was a series of unfortunate mishaps.

How could one person be so fragmented? I know it to be true that the Kingdom of God is within me, is within each one of us but yet my life is a complete catastrophe! There is a fire that smolders in my soul leaving layers of soot for me to wade through. I look back at these footprints with trepidation and curiosity. Sometimes they appear to be the size of a small child while others a grown adult. I have conducted each of my relationships with the utmost cautious maneuverings looking always to please my partner by whatever means required while my wants and needs were unimportant.

In the quiet of night when the house is without sound, children and their parents are sleeping I think. Nightfall I another one of my sweetest companion. I love the things that matter least to others like the twirling of leaves while holding on to their branches on a windy day. Knowing that Mother Nature resides in the landscape of my heart fills my pitiful life with one drop of hope. There is a life untouched within me, protected by the hand of God which covets the loss I suffered as a child. That place I went to, my spirit and soul wounded by a familiar person who stole my life by extracting the innocence I relished in.

I have spent my life struggling to escape that first nightmare and as a result have endured many unfortunate experiences. I have had to juggle both characters within while attempting to lead some semblance of an ordinary life. My being a tomboy has never been an issue between me, friends or family. That is who I have always been and it's more a reflection of my true identity then just a domineering female. I'm not afraid to be on my own away from the family since it's been my belief from long ago that I am actually an orphan or better yet adopted. I have not ever felt comfortable among my siblings except Kristopher.

It is living that grieves me most. Like a fast approaching storm filled with violence and uncertainty. In times like these I return to my childhood and reflect upon happier times when living was filled with laughter and family adventure, puppy dogs and other creatures that bring children such pleasure. I remember as a child I would see creatures with the most delicate wings as if they were angels in training. Like butterflies whose sheer wings looked as though they would melt if you dare touched them. I thought about all those times the ocean spit me out onto the shore and I would get back up and charge right back into it.

Living within walking distance to the beach, my siblings who wanted to follow us joined on for a brief journey through the San Luis Rey riverbed between our neighborhoods; Francine Villas and the barrio. We walked the few miles along with other neighborhood kids for a day at the beach during our summer breaks. When fall approaching Matthew and I would go down to the river which would be rich with pollywogs and crawfish. We loved seeking out the creatures of the environment to gaze at their beauty and indifference. I loved the texture of the horny toads and softness of the blue bellied lizards.

All God's creatures fascinated me except the bee! I am highly, no extremely allergic to their stingers and puff up like a blow fish when stung. Though I am deathly afraid of them I will avoid squashing them if I encounter one resting on the sidewalk or the road. I know they are necessary for transporting pollen from one destination to another. Our eco system would be in grave danger if ever the bee would become endangered. As much as I love the ocean it held a special and mysterious meaning for me. I braved its unruly waves and currents for as long as I could manage. I had no fear of venturing out farther then I had any business.

I secretly longed to be swept away by a passing pod of dolphins. Even though I could not swim well I still loved the challenge and how it seemed to call to me and draw me further out perhaps to test my will. I loved to watch the surfers glide through the waves with such finesse and balance. But most of all I am fascinated and bewildered by those individuals who use their bodies to shoot through the water and become one with the wave. One day I will attempt to body surf in hopes of attracting the attention of other girls like me. Athletes seem to have a pact with one another becoming friends and perhaps even lovers.

Although I managed to hide it well, I grew up an anxious child with a morbid since of being. I didn't know the rules, what or how I was supposed to act in specific situations engaging with others my age or how to interpret the actions of adults. If I had my choice, I would live in the wilderness forging my life within nature. I admire how American Indians lived their lives in nature. I believe they are the true disciples of God. They took only what they needed to survive off the land and the animals God provided for them. I love and admire also their spirituality with nature and this earth. Though it was not without trials and tribulations amongst other tribes at times, they still showed great respect for Mother Earth and all its contents.

My Grandmother is part American Indian and I hope that someday I will be able to do our family tree to find out exactly which tribe. There is so much to absorb at this point of my life. I discovered very young that there are two versions of myself and that I must nurture each one of them no matter how complex they are. All that I have learned as a child was that you could not trust anyone, that you are better off keeping an arm's length distance away from them. Allow others to come to the door but never, ever let them in. I have carried this burden like an invisible birth mark all through my life.

My traditional upbringing and deep moral and religious standards provided many a window of self expression. I often challenged the teachings not just of all God's creations but those individuals who hide behind His name. Children are His greatest glory so it states in the Bible yet they are the first to be ill treated by the very individuals who bear witness to love and protect them. Now that I am standing on my own two feet in my own space in life, I am unable to move in any direction. I know who I am, what I want but obtaining these desires is another story.

It's as though my life is fictional and I have no real meaning for existence. I have always pasted some other character into my own life because who I was has always been somewhat of a mystery. I know not what the immediate future holds for me because I haven't a clue what my purpose is. We all have choices in life as I've learned but with my life as untidy as it is my choices are limited. I don't know how to put myself first because according to family traditions and belief you do what you can for others, those less fortunate and you will reap your rewards in Heaven. That lesson was deeply rooted in not just my mind but heart as well.

I feel strongly compelled to fight for the rights of others with no voice, our children and animals alike. I am ambitious in my desires to stand up and defend those unable to stand alone or collectively as a group. I respect the rights and beliefs of others because I am not their judge. I know I have great determination in what dreams I want to pursue but my will and future are riddled with self-doubt and anxiety. I'm getting weary with the struggle to mend my shattered life. Living with a corrupted mind has caused me years of humbled distress. The impact of each experience compounded the damage even deeper.

I have forged my way through childhood disguised as outgoing, sometimes angry, and often competitive with others as well as my male siblings. I was frustrated at the lack of not understanding how it could be that my birthday was the same date as all my brothers and I yet I felt I was a fictitious character in this family. I have always felt like a boy, acted in that manner and related to everything male. It's the natural way for me. Being a tomboy was the closest I could get and it was most dissatisfying to me. I daydreamed about other girls who may share my same sentiments and feelings.

I took each disappointment personally to heart. I truly hated being a girl for so many reasons but I was in no position to change things. Besides that, what would I do? We are all born in the image of God our Father so who am I to question His decision about me? My burden in life is not about family acceptance or estrangement but the truth about myself and dealing with God. It's a relationship filled with continued turmoil and distrust. We speak everyday, when I go for walks to the park or window shopping, any time I'm alone we talk. It's a relationship I have fought to reconcile all through my life.

I know my place is not of any great importance to anyone, especially my immediate family so I have been searching to meet others like myself. It's difficult when everything you hear is negative, derogatory or repulsive comments. I believe if I had the opportunity to live my life in a natural state of existence, so many things would be different for me. Hiding each day behind someone you aren't will at some point destroy you. I'm looking for the best opportunity to share who I am with family as soon as possible. I do not know how much longer I can go on pretending.

I don't want to be looked upon with contempt or restraint. On so many levels it is said that ignorance breeds fear which breeds anger and inevitably leads to dangerous situations. I want to be set free from this dungeon I hide in. I want to be happy and create a life with someone who will support and love me for the individual I am. It is devastating to me that I haven't the strength or confidence to break away from what holds me back. Perhaps knowing the truth that nobody wants a gay child, nobody is disheartening! Everything good in my life has always been short lived or I managed to drive them away.

Perhaps it is my defense mechanism which causes me to mistreat others when they get to close or show a genuine sense of caring. At a time in my life when I could use those specific individuals now they are not available to me. Mrs. Kaahaaina whom I trust will all my heart and soul is not an option for me to share my deepest secret because I could not afford to lose her respect or love. There is gratifying solitude in being alone but the other person within isn't so comfortable with it. I pride myself on conducting my life in a responsible and independent manner but I lack the necessary confidence in pursuing my life as a single person.

Something in me believes my purpose in life is to be needed by others in order to continue living. I'm not impulsive and can't just decide to do something without first thinking about all the different ways it will affect others around me. My weaknesses outweigh my strengths two fold. I will go to any lengths to try and avoid causing anyone else pain and suffering no matter what the situation. I have suffered grievously at the loss of my dear friend Linda and I regret even to this day with deep sorrow how I wounded her. Depression is a complicated condition which I fight with on a daily basis.

I have to sacrifice my own happiness or delay it somewhat in order to protect my true identity. I've never been a person to act on my desires or wants when the opportunity presents itself. The woman at work who has flirted with me on many occasions brings my curiosity level well above the norm bit I won't respond just yet. If I could be assured God would still love me when I came out, I would do this tomorrow but He and I have a history of issues that are long from over. I decide to go home for the week-end and get a feel for how things have changed if any. I feel like a guest instead of a sibling and daughter lately.

I have been contemplating moving out from my cousin's family and in with married friends from work who have two small children. I will make my decision when I return. I call home to say I'll be in that evening after work. I took the train this time because I love trains and it's more restful then the bus even with all the frequent stops. I have had a less then successful time living up to others expectations it seems. My mother can only hope I will find a nice boy with a good job, settle down and get married, perhaps a couple of kids. It is with sincere belief that when the time comes I reveal the truth about me to her that any number of things may occur.

I have had many unpleasant experiences of rage and disorder with my mother in my lifetime so any reaction of violence or drama is highly expected. I cannot begin to assemble the right words in which to share this news so I do what I've always done on a daily basis when needing adult support. I seek the wisdom of my Heavenly Father and consult a few favorite scriptures from the good book. Even though He and I have had a volatile relationship my entire life, I've known in my heart and soul that He would never leave me. Grandma instilled that truth all through my young life that she was present in.

I knew my battle could be a long one if I didn't get this situation taken care of as soon as I settled in for the long week-end. The train stopped at every station along the coast south bound and I liked to think it would be the longest ride of my life. Nothing I did or said came easy. I was always thinking about how my decision to come out would affect the family, my friends and most importantly my relationship with Mrs. Kaahaaina. I wasn't a significant role model any longer with my siblings or even my mother for that matter so losing favor with them wasn't a big deal. I have always felt more like an orphan that family member anyway.

I've lived my entire life behind an immensely thick shield of armor and not too much bothered or stuck to me of people's opinions. I kept my head held high knowing that only God had the right to judge and as long as I treated others decently, with respect and compassion then I would do alright. I had a high price to pay for my already devastating misfortunes with others but I was making an effort to repair those deficiencies. I knew I would seek or attempt to seek the assistance of our family therapist so that gave me some comfort. I needed to find a way, a means for standing up to the dominant character within me.

I was at the worst odds I could possibly be in and I desperately needed someone to tell me it was alright to be a lesbian. It is a difficult description to use for me because it isn't quite who or what I identified with. I feel more like an asexual individual then having to pick one of those truly uncomfortable adjectives. I don't see myself as female, male or somewhere in-between. I am empathetic to any society who suffers injustice and persecutions for their differences. It's been a lifelong quest beginning in grade school defending those childhood friends and acquaintances that were picked on by the stronger more domineering kids.

I was fortunate enough that being a tomboy afforded me a following that others knew not to bother. I was not afraid to defend myself or those close to me. My friends could count on me in any situation. That vein of anger was aroused on more then once occasion for which I was well within my rights not to be accused of starting or provoking the drama. Colleen and I had come close to physical altercations on several occasions but I knew better then to lay a hand on her no matter how she tempted me. Restrain was a behavior that needed a lot of attention I was aware.

By the time the train arrived in Oceanside after the noon hour I wasn't surprised that the parking lot was empty of any familiar faces. I would wait no longer then fifteen minutes before I took the mile or so hike over to the house on Holly Street. I only brought home the minimum apparel for the week-end and some money for expenses. I don't make a lot by any standards but I manage to put a portion away by automatic deduction to the credit union account I started when I first got hired. Aunt Connie gave me some good advice about what I should do first above all else with my pay check.

I appreciated her advice since I was the worst when it came to finances. We were never taught anything about money or how to handle it since we never really had any to speak about. Of course we had our allowances before dad left us but then money was always so scarce and rarely did we have any extra. Mom did her best to supplement dad's child support checks but raising three growing girls is tough even for two parent homes. I felt it was my obligation to pitch in and do whatever I could to help. I usually took care of the girls needs by providing clothes or something they really needed that mom couldn't give them.

I always made sure I kept enough money on me for a ticket and a phone call. I didn't understand the concept of the value of money or how to manage it for later in life for whatever might come along. I have neither worldly expectations nor enthusiasm to live for any extended period of time beyond the present. I do not bother to waste my time thinking about what I will do next or where will I be five, ten years from now. I still have some difficulty thinking past the day. Surviving this long has been more mental torture then I care to live with. My fascination with committing suicide is never further then a blink away.

It is the only sure act that would bring me peace of mind. I have been deprived of an ordinary life since that horrific experience at age three and all others thereafter. As hard as I try, I cannot escape my past no matter what I do to keep me pre occupied. I don't want to be lonely any more and I don't want to continue living an obvious lie. It's against everything I believe in to pretend being something I'm not. I have so many places to hide that the average person would not know my smile wasn't entirely genuine. I force myself to act happy and pretend that everything is going just fine because you need no explanation for a jubilant disposition.

The last place I want to be is swirling around in a life of turmoil. I have had enough of that and it's time to move on. The only issue now is that my heart and head cannot find a meaningful compromise between sitting down for a family talk or just tell mom and see how she reacts. The constant battle between the two doesn't help either. I need to be sure myself that this is not a condition which can be cured or turned around with years of aggressive therapy or medication like I hear and read about all the time. It is an emotional topic to say the least and I have to speak from my heart for that is where God resides.

If no one else, I know that He will never deny me because of whom and what I am. I have been practicing this speech inside my head for so long now that it should be easy to convey. My biggest enemy is that I have always taken into consideration what effect my telling will have on others. I don't know how not to feel for others first no matter what my consequences. It's a shame there has been nobody I could truly trust with this information. It will surely alter the relationships I have with everybody I tell. So either way it seems the cost to me is definitely higher.

Summer would trudge by slowly as I approached the busy streets heading towards the house with my little suitcase in tow. Crossing Hill Street towards Saint Mary's Star of the Sea Church where I had made my First Holy Communion as a child brought back bitter sweet memories. I knew it would not take me long to reach the house as I moved swiftly through town. Crossing Horne street to take the shortcut behind the shopping center and through the East side barrio was never a problem for me like it was for those skeptical of it's reputation for not being fond of Anglo Saxon kids.

People in this neighborhood knew me and my relatives from way back so there was no fear of being looked down upon or intimidated. I was not afraid of the gangs of any color. I simply moved along like I belonged there and waved to school mates or their parents when I passed their houses. Balderamma Park was notorious for being unfriendly or even dangerous at certain times of the night but I still had no fear. My siblings are well known and they know who I am as well.

Once I reached the corner of Holly and San Diego Street I was five minutes from the house. I could see no car in the drive and knew mom was not there.

I pulled the house key out of my right pants pocket and opened the door. I felt eerie entering the empty house as the quiet blanketed me. The smell of pinto beans cooking comforted me. I looked around to see how the house had changed since it had been a few weeks of my last visit. I suddenly felt a wave of sadness as I peered at the family pictures hanging in the hallway. The tears welled up in my eyes and echoed loudly in my mind as they hit the linoleum floor between my feet. We were all smiling in every picture no matter what the occasion. So much has transpired in our lives since each of these pictures was taken and I miss how close we once were.

The girls were settled in their room and mom in her's. Matthew was either at work or with his friend Richard. If I decided to return back home different sleeping arrangements would have to be made. I proceeded to clean up a bit and put the dishes in the sink away. I thought I would take everyone out for pizza at Filippi's, our favorite place across from Oceanside High School where Colleen attends. No sooner do I finish in the bathroom then I hear familiar voices in the living room. I see the girls coming through the door with their hands full of grocery bags and Mom close behind. We exchange smiles and say hello as I go over to help.

Mom says she couldn't remember what time I was arriving and apologized for not being there to pick me up. I nodded it was alright and continued helping the girls unload the food. She say's she was making my favorite dinner of empanadas, beans and fedo. I smiled as I thought about all the times we had disagreed about one thing or another and how one of us always left the scene highly agitated slamming doors on the way out. Our disruptive displays of anger were healthy for no one least of all my sisters. Our relationship from the start of my school years has always been filled with hostility and discontent.

I didn't want our relationship to remain shattered but it will no doubt take some work on both our sides. I will make the effort as I have in the past because I was taught by Grandmother whether I liked it or not. You only have one mother and therefore one must ultimately make unpleasant sacrifices at times to sustain the relationship until a time when you separate yourself from their presence or control by becoming a responsible, self sufficient adult. My only problem with this is that I started making those sacrifices when the family began dissolving after Grandma died and dad left.

I don't want to be a part of the incomplete puzzle of our lives. I want us to regain the need for one another and be at least friends. I look around my relatives lives and see how they manage to deal with their own struggles but remain faithful to the family. I need to belong to a family who will love and nourish me until the day I die. How does one possibly move past a catastrophe such as sexual abuse when she has no one to trust? I cannot afford to or am not willing to lose the only person whom sustains my hopes in life, Mrs. Kaahaaina. It brings me no comfort in knowing I do not know her well enough to believe she will continue to love me no matter what I am.

I have the greatest respect for her and her husband Dave so I can't risk losing that. God and I speak everyday and yet I cannot say for sure He isn't disappointed as well. I just want to do the right thing and not hurt or bring anymore pain to anyone's life as I know the possibility is real for mom. She didn't do well when Kammillie dated boys of color so I can expect this displeasure to fall in the same category. There are no plans for doing anything special for Fourth of July so we'll just hang out here and more likely then not be able to see an array of fireworks from all around the city including the High School and the Harbor.

We don't have the best seats in town but once we sit on the roof the view is better. I did what I could to help with dinner, rolling out the tortilla dough and feeding them to mom so she could stuff them with the ingredients she cooked up. The fedo was easy to make and beans would be refried just as the rest of the meal was being placed in there serving dishes. This is the kind of food I grew up with and missed it a great deal. Cousin Cecelia makes one of the easiest dishes I've ever had and insist she make it at least once a day when I spend time with her and the three kids, Michael seven and Gabriella three and Danny will be two in September.

I have to admit that I feel more comfortable; more accepted in my cousin's families then my own. Even though I have suffered unbearably at the hands of my Uncle in the past my desire to belong to this pod of family is stronger then ever before. I see how they have troubles but stick together and manage to work through the difficult times. I wanted my family to be that strong, to want to stay together and work out the problems. Unfortunately things didn't go that way and how tragic our reality has become. I yearned for a companion like I had in Kristopher and a Grandmother who loved me just the way I was.

I look around the table as everyone is talking, telling their story and how the summer is going. I am happy to see mom is still dating, glad that the men are more her age. I couldn't tell if she was ever going to remarry and so the question rises once again; when do I stop taking care of the family in pursuit of doing things for myself? It is a dilemma that haunts me without mercy. When do my obligations stop and my life begin? They'll always be my family, unable to disconnect them like an electrical cord from the outlet. There are some things in life that are a right of passage and cannot be so easily discarded and family is number 1.

We spend the long week-end hanging out around the house and a day at the beach where I questioned the girls how mom was doing in my absence. Perhaps it was a silly inquiry but I needed to know for myself. While mom had gone out with her girlfriends for the evening I made my questions brief trying to get a feel of whether I should return or not and what impact it would have on them as well. I have been gone from home since last November and so much has changed. They have adjusted to my absence and although I could detect a bit of strain in Michele's voice when it came to Colleen I would make a point to talk to her further later on.

Colleen and I have always lived with a touch of tension between us from early childhood for reason's unknown to me. She is the closest and most protective of mom out of all us girls. She isn't very nice to Michelle either but I suppose that could be a big sister, little sister thing. Michelle appears to be a bit timid at times more often then not and I wish I was around more to protect her. I'm a little disappointed that neither of them asked how I have been doing or want to know what it's like living away from home. I was however excited just a little when Michelle asked if she could come back with me sometime.

I told her she could come anytime so long as she had mom's permission. I promised her I would bring her as soon as I could and I knew it would be alright with any of our cousin's and Aunt Connie. Life could be tricky for Michelle because she isn't strong and is easily hurt by other's comments or perceptions of her. As for Colleen and I have we have pretty thick skin and don't really give a crap what people think? As much alike as we are, there are some definite differences in our character. In spite of all our misgivings I am fiercely protective of them both and will do anything necessary to defend them if needed.

Even though I didn't spend much time alone with mom and thus was unable to talk to her about my coming out I assessed the situation as close as possible and determined that it would happen on one of my future visits this summer. Colleen informed me that she was seeing the same therapist mom was and I let her know that I would like to meet this woman and speak to her about nothing in particular but just to get a feel for what she's like. Obviously I have an ulterior motive but this was neither here nor there. I told the girls if there was anything they might need or want to please let me know and I would do everything I could to get it for them.

I didn't call or try to reach any of my friends on this trip as it was important to me to try and get mom alone to speak with her. As always she's in another place and was unavailable to talk this time around. I was not completely surprised or disappointed that this trip did not accomplish what I had set out to but I know the opportunity is coming around and I look forward to the exchange of conversation it will surely bring. I've found out that they've gotten along fine without me all these month's. Whether they want to admit it or not for fear of hurting my feelings or damaging our relationship in any way, life does go on, with or without me.

I set aside the issues of home for now on my way back to Glendale after mom and the girls dropped me off. This was not as productive as I had hoped between mom and I but on the other hand I was more successful with the girls in finding out how they felt. My next decision was dealing with the intention of moving out of my cousin's home and in with some friends from work, Luisa and Thwat with their two small children Boyd and Renee. They have a nice size house in the valley and Luisa's sister and husband also share their home. She is from Lubbock Texas and he is from Thailand, a very nice guy.

She had asked if I would be interested in coming to live with them as a live in sitter on the side. I told her I would think about it and let her know. With everything going on in my life it might be the best thing for me to do right now separating myself from the family entirely. Certainly I will miss Betty and the kids; little Richard, Anthony and Lacy. They are a bundle of joy and filled with so much excitement that I feel I'm intruding at times and they have no privacy. I stay on the couch because it is only a two bedroom but I don't mind. It will be nice to have a room of my own.

I had made a very bad decision lately and felt very ashamed of my actions so it just seems right that I move on and not continue feeling the guilt of my mistake. I have been with them since last November and so much has happened that has been good for me in some respect but also a thing or two which was unfortunate. Overall we will always remain family and I shall be indebted especially to Betty for all she did for me. I love the kids and will miss them dearly but we will continue to see one another and visit on some week-ends. It's funny how much in common Betty and I have and I secretly hope one day I can talk to her about myself.

She is more like a big sister then my cousin's wife and I love her dearly. I hope the rest of my cousin's won't be upset that I'm moving on but I will continue to see and call them on the phone. For so many reasons I will change my landscape just to see what life could be like away from all family on a daily basis. I remember fondly our trips to local parks playing football and barbecuing or horseback riding for the afternoon. It was a family event for everyone and it's what they did together as often as they could. Richard has his own Plumbing business with a partner Oscar, his best friend.

My stay here has been lifesaving to say the least even when I had my own issues to deal with. Being around the children always brought me peace and comfort. For me children are the truest of solace. They keep me happy and content, make me laugh and bring a joy like no other feeling in the world. I need a little happiness in my life right now and moving on seems the right choice for me to make. I will tell them at work Monday and discuss this with Richard and Betty when I return. All this thinking has exhausted me as I try and clear my mind the rest of the ride home.

Glendale could be a very nice place to start a new life. Nobody knows me and any women I meet will be perfect strangers where as I would be able to be myself if I felt strong enough about them. Upon my return I was picked up by Aunt Connie and Uncle Felix. I felt quite uneasy about the ride home as there was an issue unresolved of late. My financial situation had been in question and there were long conversations about how I divvied up my weekly funds. The point at the end of the evening was that I would be responsible for any misgivings and make the appropriate adjustments to console the situation.

It was in that moment I decided to tell Luisa that I would be glad to move in with them if they were still interested in having me. I don't own much and anything I have could be packed in my trunk and hauled to their house. I spoke to Richard and Betty briefly about my decision and the response was mixed. They loved having me around even if it meant losing some privacy but there were other issues surrounding my exit that I would not discuss. It was best that I leave while things were okay between us. My drinking was out of control and they weren't entirely aware of how I use to sneak alcohol.

I need to be on my own away from any family no matter how unpleasant it would be in the beginning. I was truly unhappy about my weight and the drinking didn't help! I didn't even like the taste of it but it got me through the emotional turmoil. I was still torn between family and self, life and death. Love and happiness have always been an illusion for me. I wasn't schooled on having expectations of either myself or life. My options were very minimal to say the least. I have been confined to an existence exclusively harbored within the dungeon of my soul. My reality I could not reveal to anyone.

Only God knew my secrets and even He and I have intermittent communications at times. We have an understanding between us and it is faith alone and an instinctive well of belief that there is a real reason I am still here. My purpose in this life is unknown to me yet its there, sure as I know God stands right beside me always no matter what state of mind I'm in. I know from past experiences that no matter how tremendously bad life gets, I never walk alone. Just like Mr. Jerry Lewis says on his Muscular Dystrophy telethons with tears in his eyes and voice cracking, *our struggles are never alone.*

It's extremely uneasy to be the type of person I am in these uncertain times. I have been dancing closer with death these past few years with much less armor then ever. My life I feel is going into a frenzy that I cannot control nor subdue. At this moment of my life I feel like I'm at the starting gate of a deep hidden psychological nightmare. The summer of purgatory is upon me. I sometimes feel I've gone to sea with a cement life preserver. Dealing with depression has always been a hidden character of mine yet I've somehow managed to get through it. Perhaps my will is stronger then I realize.

I can live with just about anybody and be myself to a certain extent but the truth of being a lesbian opens an umbrella of emotions. I'm at an intersection with making the decision that I have always struggled with all through my life. I feel comfortable around these new friends but uncertain how they feel about people like me. I simply am unable to translate who I am inside and live freely without one ounce of shame. Me, myself and I are at a crucial impasses and a life altering transition must take place in order for me, Miracle to exist. My deep rooted anxiety is not the pain my mom or siblings may suffer but more my relationship with God, my Father.

Standing on the edge of suicide is boring me. Fear, disgust and anger have complicated matters for me in exposing my truth, my reality. I have seen how society is unkind to indifference, especially one such as mine. Although homosexuality has been in existence since the beginning of man it is still the lifestyle most repulsive to mainstream America. I will not apologize for who or what I am to anybody but I must be completely aware of the consequences at such an exposing truth. As if that isn't enough to keep me from coming out, I am still suffocating at the controlling hands and emotions of guilt and shame.

That in turn makes me angrier which creates an utterly hopeless situation. On one hand I'm fighting for my life to move on and find a way to get past this but underneath the skin a volcano is about to erupt and I haven't a clue where to go or what to do. I can see my doom approaching rapidly without regard for things around me which I could use as shelter from such storms. I have two prominent veins; one which is streaming with deep insecurity and the other with an immeasurable amount of faith. My crisis remains that how do I go about separating them?

My childhood experiences have left me disabled in so many crippling ways that I chose to live in the solitude of my soul. It's still the safest retreat I know. Madness is a reality I know lives behind one of the few doors that occupy the landscape of my mind. I could not escape to much longer from pretending it was not there. My life to this point has been a collage of failed relationships and social isolation. I loved school because I was in a controlled environment and thus unable to go outside the boundaries of walls I had constructed. It was imperative I keep each one of me in perspective.

Moving into an unfamiliar environment with Luisa, her children and sister could be good for me. Their children are very cute and friendly so that should work out just fine. I know they spend a lot of time with family on both sides so meeting new people from a different culture is rather exciting for me as well. It will help keep my mind off personal issues. When work commenced and all returned to normal I got together with Luisa and we decided the following weekend would be best to use her cousin's truck to come get my trunk. I didn't want to move out while the kids were there so it was decided Richard, Betty and the kids would spend the day doing family stuff.

There was some degree of anxiety but this had to be done, I would leave my phone number and address. I was hoping this would be a positive separation and that nobody would be hurt, least of all the kids. Work resumed and the week passed by quickly but not soon enough for me. The others in our work area knew I was moving in with them and their feelings were mixed but I didn't care one way or the other how people felt. One of the awful things about working in factories is the degree of gossip that goes around at any given time. I was fortunate in that I didn't know these people and therefore cared even less of their opinions.

I didn't like when my peers came up to me and warned me about the woman who expressed an interest in meeting with me after work some day for coffee or breakfast some week-end morning. Inside I wanted to find a way to pass her my phone number but didn't know how without people finding out. Aunt Connie worked in the building north of mine and I would go visit her on either breaks or at lunch. It took about a week or so to get settled in and the kids and I are getting along just fine. Her husband Thwat is a thin man with a ferocious appetite. I loved the type of food they ate even though it was quite hot. I hadn't had curry before but I liked it.

I didn't cut back on my drinking any but I also wouldn't indulge when the kids were around. They are a busy clan visiting friends or relatives practically every week-end. When the men went to the temple the women would do their own things. Most of the time I would stay home with the two kids while Luisa went out and did whatever. I loved their company and the oldest, Renee was such the entertainer. Soon enough life became a routine like any other and I took a walk one day up to the school yard where people were playing softball. I walked around the neighborhood often as to not be idle at home.

In one of these games I was approached by a guy who asked if I would be interested in joining the team. It was a co-ed league which started in a couple weeks. I expressed an interest and told him I would be at their next practice. I watched a little longer to see what caliber players I was dealing with and felt I could be an asset. He told me most of the kids were still in High school and I mentioned I had just graduated this past June. There were no age restrictions but he did prefer to have a team with well dispersed players of the same talent. I assured him I'd be equal or better then the men.

Even though I had gained more weight then I have ever carried in my life, I knew I was still capable of playing with these folks without any problem. It was an incentive to give up the liquor and get back in shape. It was the end of July by now and I had met a rather frisky young girl named Tracy on the team who seemed awful curious about me. She was a sophomore at the local High school and was trying out for the same team. I was hesitant at first of her advances but realized soon afterwards she was just having some teenage fun. I did everything I could to contain my excitement around her even when she displayed playful wrestling.

I wasn't quite sure what her motives were as she continued to paw and attempt to kiss me on occasion while we wrestled around in her front yard. I had met her parents and little brother. They appear to be a nice loving family and I would not disrespect them by taking advantage of their daughter's forwardness. I had to think of it like she was just a teenager exploring. I would not allow myself to put my guard down and give her any leeway. Although I adored the attention she was showing me I couldn't bring myself to give in no matter how difficult she was making it. Her endless enthusiasm and non stop energy reminded me of how I use to be.

She may have been curious but I don't know her that well and to be intimate with someone her age would be dangerous for me. Life moves along slowly and I was settled in at the house. Week-ends varied from visiting friends, staying home to watch the kids or shopping. I had a visit or two from my former companion whom I had intimate relations with but I ended it after the second time which I simply could no longer comply. He was married with children and frankly, sleeping with a man was the most repulsive act I could participate in. I told him not to call me ever again or try to see me otherwise. It was the last time I saw him after that.

The month of August swooped in like a giant gust of wind. Work was going fine, my little girlfriend was still around and life in West Hollywood was exciting. There was lots of news about the upcoming Gay Pride Parade which I wish I could attend but nobody in the household was any wiser of my truth. It was for the better I felt since I was a guest in their home and I couldn't afford to bring any unpleasant situations into their home. I had something else to ponder over concerning a friend of the families who was looking to marry an American girl so he could get his green card.

Although they approached me with the promise of a rather large fee to marry him with the stipulation there would be no sex or obligation to remain married after the short period of time needed for him to acquire his green card and eventually his citizenship. My concern was that I don't speak the language and therefore it would be impossible for us to communicate and what would the living arrangements be? There were many questions to be answered even before I could consider it but the ten thousand dollars was something I could really use. He wasn't a bad looking guy even though he stood over six feet tall. His moon shaped face with bid dark eyes complemented by a wide smile.

He too was from Thailand and seemed very pleasant. There was no pressure just that I think about it. He currently is a student here at the University but wanted to become a citizen. If I was a different kind of woman there would be no question but I'm not. I enjoyed the company of my little friend whom lately has been getting friskier by the visit! I decide that the next time she attempts to steal a kiss, I won't stop her. I won't provoke her any further but I will not prevent her from getting what she's after. I like how I feel around her, the fun we have rolling around the grass and trying to see who's stronger.

I so want to let myself go with her but I won't, I can't. That self discipline and knowledge that I must act responsibly will surely kick in and I will be regretting in for the rest of the summer. She may be young but she's awful forward for someone her age! I liked it but I wouldn't lead her on. I'm like the big sister that say's enough is enough and settle down! If she only knew how desperately I wanted to let all my inhibitions go! Days pasted into weeks and no sooner then August had begun then it was on its way out. There was a birthday party we were invited to for one of Luisa's nephews just around the corner from the house.

I didn't do well at parties filled with strangers and people I didn't know. Her cousin would be there and I knew her fairly well but she would be the only one other then Luisa, Thwat, her sister and husband and the kids. I felt reluctant but I still went. Most of the kids are my age some in some out of High school but all quite friendly. Within the hour the backyard and house were overflowing with teenagers and nearly as many parents. I stuck to the kids like glue while Luisa and the other adults mingled with their friends. Chatter filled the air mingled with music fighting for ear space.

A little ways into the celebration there was some commotion coming from the front of the house and I went to the side fence to see what was going on. I heard cars screech to a halt and car doors slam. I felt something was going wrong or about to when I watched as a group of guys dressed in dark clothing approached some of the kids from the party who were gathered in the front yard. Fighting commenced all of a sudden and everything was happening so fast I couldn't react! There was some yelling and raised voices which had caught the attention of others in the backyard.

I jumped off the fence and looked for Thwat to tell him something was going on out front. It was as if simultaneously all the adult males took off like a flock pf seagulls and ran through the house to investigate. I spotted Luisa and her sister with the other women and walked towards her. She looked at me with her big black eyes and asked what was going on? As I started to tell her what I heard and saw the men were coming back in the side gate huddled around a couple of the kids from the party. Apparently there was a rival gang who wanted to crash the party and the boys told them it was private or something to that effect.

Typically this is a safe neighborhood that watched out for one another but like any neighborhood anywhere in these United States, gangs are everywhere and they all have their own agenda. The house was the only one on the street celebrating but not loudly or out of control. It was pretty much confined to the backyard and house. After a few minuets of discussion between the young boys and men some of them left the party in pursuit of these kids whom the boys recognized. Thwat and his circle of friends are a very close, tight knit group who not only go to temple for worship often but also play basketball together as well. They are all like brothers.

After we had gone home later that evening Thwat asked me how come I didn't come to them sooner, why didn't I come right away? I didn't like his insinuations that I took my sweet time to get help! I told him it all happened so fast that I didn't know right off they were fighting! Those kids would be dealt with when the time and place were right. I felt bad for the boys but they defended themselves as vigorously as they could far as I could see before I left to tell Thwat. The thing is there very protective of their family and don't take kindly to intruders. I knew it was a matter of time before they dealt with those boys.

The week end went on uneventful as we stayed around the house and watched sports all day Sunday. I was glad that they were big football fans and I loved my Pittsburg Steelers. Although I was an Oceanside native I wasn't a fan of the local team the Chargers. I enjoyed watching the brutality of the Oakland Raiders and other fiercely physical teams. I D always wished they had women's professional football teams because I'd be the first one to sign up! With the month of August coming to an end soon it would be time for my little friend to get back to school.

I didn't make the softball team I started out for because some week-ends I would be home and they would be playing ball. I wasn't that committed like when I'm home so that kind of fell by the wayside. I was still uncertain where my future would be but for now I was trying to save up enough money to buy a good used car. Richard had asked me earlier in the year that if I wanted to but his 69 Firebird that he would give to me with the understanding that it needed a new engine. I loved his orange with white interior convertible. I use to love sitting in the front seat on drives when Betty would take the kids and me to McDonalds for lunch.

I planned to go back home for a visit the week before the girls went back to school and buy them some school clothes or anything else they needed. I have enjoyed my stay here with Luisa and her family. Her daughter Renee is a mirror image of her father, thin and tall for her age with waist long dark brown hair and beautiful almond shaped brown eyes. Her smile was just like her fathers and she was such a prissy little thing, a true definition of a girl. While on the other side is her little brother Boyd. He is a wild and rambunctious little boy who likes being with his parents every waking minute.

I love being a part of their happiness and they certainly bring enormous joy to my life. I played with the kids anytime they wanted me to swing them around by their arms in mid air and then let them try and stand up. I don't know who got more dizzy, them or me! I've stopped drinking after an incident with my boss who tried to feel me up one evening on our way home from a party we had with others from work. It started out as happy hour and they had to sneak me in which a small amount of money was exchanged so long as we stayed in the furthest back of the club away from the general population. I wasn't allowed to drink but I did steal a few gulps when people went to the bathroom.

When it was time to go back to Oceanside the kids asked if I could bring back one of my sisters. I told them I would come back with a surprise. I had enough money saved to get both of the girls something for school. I saved up two hundred dollars each and figured that should help a little. I didn't know the style or what kids were wearing these days but I knew my sisters weren't in to fancy labels or high end clothes or shoes. They usually got hand me downs so I wanted to get them their own new clothes. Now that I was out of school my wardrobe consisted of Levis, tee shirts, sweatshirts and Stan Smith tennis shoes.

Name brands were for the wealthy and upper class folks. I loved my Levis and shirts. I was a very simply, low maintenance kind of person who didn't care for fancy. Besides that, I couldn't afford the prices of Reebok, Nike or all the other over priced shoes and apparel. I preferred sandals or flip flops to shoes any day. I reserved my visit to the needs of my sisters and not idle conversation with mom. I would have to cross that bridge at another date. Once again I arrived at the bus station with nobody waiting for me. I don't know why I expected this time to be any different!

How hard was it for them to be there when I only came home once a month? I still always hoped that just once they might surprise me. I called but nobody answered so I made my little trek home and got there about thirty minutes later. I walked fast because I grew up with a tall brother, Matthew and in order to walk anywhere with him you had to keep up with those mile long legs and that wide stride. Once again the house was empty but the television was on so that was a sign they would be back soon. The house didn't look much different then my last visit so I looked around inside and out then sat on the couch and waited.

Once they arrived shortly afterwards they had said they went down to pick me up but realized they had missed me when they went to check the schedule. It was all insignificant at this point. I just wanted to get the girls to the shopping center or wherever they wanted to go. Mom said she would drop us off and pick us up when we were ready to come home. I was glad she wasn't going to stay with us. I needed the company of my sisters without the presence of the parent to influence their purchases so I could get to know them a little bit. I was afraid of losing their support. I wouldn't run out on them like Kammillie did me.

Even if I didn't come back, they would always be welcome in my home wherever I lived. I was just a visitor now and it really didn't matter one way or the other how they felt. They had adjusted to my absence and managed to get along without me. There really was no place here for me and the sooner I accepted that reality the sooner I could start my life on my own. I missed them desperately but it appears those feelings aren't mutual. I asked Colleen if she continued going to her therapist and she said yes. I expressed that I still wanted to meet her sometime and she said whenever I came down during the week or stayed over on a Monday.

I would see what I could do but let her know when that would be. Colleen is going to be a sophomore this year and Michelle in seventh grade at Jefferson Junior High School. I thought about Mrs. Snyder instantaneously and wondered if she would have her as a P. E. teacher. I would inquire at a later date when she's been at school a few weeks. I was excited for them both because I have always been a huge fan of education and staying in school. If I was smart, I would have gone in the service and got a free education. September is a pretty time of year and starting to get much cooler.

We spent all afternoon shopping at the mall in Carlsbad and having lunch. It was quite a successful day for me and I was thankful that the girls appeared to have fun. They each got a few outfits and school supplies which I knew would help mom out a great deal. Buying clothes and supplies is an expense difficult for her because she is on a limited budget and self supporting. We called to mom know she were ready and in the meanwhile talked about what they were looking forward to in school. Michelle was anxious to meet back up with old friends and Colleen was anxious to play sports. The whole experience was pleasant and uplifting.

I missed them and was torn about whether or not to return. The importance of family overshadowed any thoughts about self satisfaction or preservation. My family comes first and foremost. The ride home allowed me to think deeply about how to determine what my next move would be. I needed to save as much money as I could and when would I return, end of the year, next year? I cannot say at this moment but I shall give it some serious thought. I suppose I could find a job without any problem since there are plenty of factories in our area. I would like to earn enough money to buy myself a car so I could be independent of mom.

I would see how my housemates felt about my leaving and see if there is any support there. It hasn't been easy for me to make decisions about what I want to do for myself compared to family obligations. In spite of how they feel, I must take an approach that will benefit the family as a whole. I sincerely hope that mom will marry her boyfriend which would alleviate the stress I have for making my own way. She doesn't need a man to take care of her that would never suffice. She is fiercely independent and has too much pride to fall dependent on another man.

She has her own wants and needs that I see conflict one another but who am I to tell her this? Our relationship has a lot to be desired and most of the time is strained for one reason or another but I must think about the effect it has on my siblings. The question remains; how would my coming back change the landscape of the family unit? When it comes to love and family expectations, I fail at defending my dreams to pursue the goals I set. School was a safe haven and island of solitude but it does not pay the bills. This is why the military is such an attractive, obvious solution.

There is so much to think about that it drains me. We pull into the bus depot and I find my way off the bus and search the crowd for Luisa and the kids. I find comfort in knowing that whenever I arrive back here someone is always waiting for me. Their smiley little faces as they run towards me and I reach down to scoop them up. It's quite an emotional rollercoaster for me to be surrounded by children and not have any of my own. I tried so desperately in High School with Mark but without success. I don't know if it was a message from God that it's not my calling to be a mother or what.

I am a fierce protector of all children if our entire family from siblings, nephews and nieces all the way through to cousins. I am grateful that we have such a large extended family, I just wish we all got together more often like when we were younger. But people grow up, move on and move away. My heart strings are not as flexible as the others in my family. All the self confidence I have is stored behind a door in the attic of my mind. On our ride home the kids talked about what they did all week-end, played at their cousin's house and ate a lot of food while Daddy watched sports on television and played basketball with his friends.

They asked me what I did and I told them how I took my sisters shopping for school clothes and such and that I had a nice visit. Renee asked me if any of them would come up for a visit before school started. I told her Colleen would come the following week or week after. I just had to make sure and call her to do anything I had to getting her up here. The bus ticket was no problem but whether or not she would want to come was another story. We haven't always been friends but I know if I explained the situation she would agree. Perhaps mom could drive up and visit her sister then we would go get her.

They were plans not entirely impossible but I needed to verify everything. I would take a nap once we got home and call Colleen later that evening. The house smelled of the wonderful aromas of curry and chicken cooking in the kitchen. I loved the food they made because it was so different then anything I was use to, hot and spicy but very good. I would not allow myself to show how uncomfortable and miserable I was while consuming it but it never stopped me from continuing to eat. I would suffer afterwards each time but then again it was well worth it. Nothing a few Tums couldn't cure.

It was difficult to close my eyes for any length of time in the beginning as the kids came in and wanted to nap with me but found out immediately it was their ploy to engage me in wrestling about! I so enjoyed their company that I could not deny them their fun and therefore tickled them profusely, got them in bear hugs so they could not escape and struggled and tussled with them until they got quite exhausted from it. Mom came along and insisted they let me rest and dragged them from the room. I know I would miss them dearly. My brief conversation with Colleen was successful as I explained the situation and promised she would be up in a week or two.

After a short conversation with mom telling her I would send them gas money everything was a go and they would be up Labor Day week-end. We would go to one of the cousin's houses, Richard and Betty's or Cecilia's and Octavo's for the family gathering. There was no negative outfall for my leaving after we discussed the situation and they understood so things we're good between us. I was looking forward to yet another family bash like the old days. I didn't think it would be an opposition to bring Luisa, Thwat and the two kids along to officially meet everybody. I think mom will like them, especially Luisa.

For the next two weeks life resumed, work went on eight hours a day back and forth from Glendale to West Hollywood up and down a crowded highway five days a week. I was still uncomfortable with the weight I was carrying even though I had lost five to ten pounds but it was still uncomfortable. I know that my eating habits are primarily emotional driven and when I'm unhappy to the point of depressed my eating plummets. I consume more alcohol even though it is a hidden vice that I have managed to curb lately, it still occurs. I know it won't be allowed openly when I return back home and that's alright with me.

I plan on going back to school and research the possibility of working for the East County chapter of Hope which is a facility I believe that houses or cares for abused, sick and or neglected children. I like to believe that my purpose or at least my calling has something to do directly with children of that environment and nature. Mom has worked in Head Start for some years now and I have enjoyed my visits whenever I would go see how the classroom is conducted. I am ashamed that I'm not bilingual but that is something I can correct by taking classes night school at my old High School.

Until I find out what's really important to me I will investigate returning to school and taking some courses in child psychology and doing home study on the different conditions of childhood like autism and attention deficit disorders. Children are my focus exclusively and whether I go to get my teaching credentials for secondary education or counselor it's what interests me now. I may not have any children on my own but like Mrs. Kaahaaina told me when we first met and

I inquired as to why she didn't have any children she replied that her students were her children and she was perfectly happy that way.

I would never let go of the fantasy that some day they would adopt me away from my family that I really felt no part of. I have always been an orphan in that family and nothing I ever did or said made any difference or was appreciated by any of them. It's what was expected I suppose through out a history of family traditions. I missed grandmother deeply and longed to find consolation with anyone as wise. For many reason's I was not just hesitant about returning back home but severely resentful to myself that I could not breakaway from the family who had clearly learned to live without my presence.

Why do I insist on punishing myself this way I cannot understand. Perhaps it will take my seeking the assistance of a therapist to set myself free. I am more then willing to share all my pain and misery once I find that threshold of trust with her if I am able. Come Friday of Labor Day week-end I prepare my surrogate family of the involvement of my family and that they do not have to stay for any length of time. We would pick up Colleen for a day or two for her visit and see how things go. I didn't want to share any other information about the family and let them make their on conclusions.

We would bring along soft drinks and a couple dishes for the barbecue as there would be plenty of children present. I sincerely miss all of my cousin's and when I saw them again I was filled with remorse. There was a drive in me so deep to take Cecilia aside and confide my transgressions in her that it was hurtful to keep silent. I had a lifetime of experience hiding in the dungeon of my soul and thus able to continue in public as if everything was fine. The torture inside was an entirely different story. My Aunt Connie and Uncle Felix were just as happy to see me as well as I introduced Luisa, Thwat and their kids to everybody who was present.

I informed them before hand that we would not be staying as long as the others and that Colleen was going to spend a day or two with me but that she would be returned in time to head back with mom and Michele. Everyone mingled with one another and the kids had a blast playing with one another as well. I missed this whole scene and was reminded of years in my childhood when we use to do this often each summer at either Tamarack beach in Carlsbad or the Harbor in Oceanside. It was a very sentimental experience for me but one I absorbed and set inside the storage of my soul. Matthew didn't join this trip because he was working.

I wanted these times back as regular as they could occur but everybody knows that's not always easily planned. Mom is in the middles of relatives with half being up here and the other in San Diego. Our entire family visits are to far and few between and I'm afraid that that's just how life progresses. People's lives are developing all around me while I remain dormant in the dungeon of my soul not matter how I struggle to get past it, to move and pursue my own life, I allow myself to be defeated by family traditions, expectations and duties as the oldest child to help preserve the family and offer my assistance as I am able.

I don't know how to behave otherwise. I had no immediate family mentor's aside from Kristopher whom has been gone five years now that would teach me successful life lessons from money matters to self expression. There was no future to save for or dream about to be honest. It was all a ploy for me that I might gain some want or learn some meaningful purpose for my existence. Death was still my closest companion and it was only a matter of time when we would conclude that at this appointed time and date I would move on to a higher, hopefully more gratifying plane of existence.

There was never really any family support for us kids to express our goals or attain our dreams. Most of our friends lived a life I dreamed about with a complete family with a two parent home. Mother had lots of boyfriends since dad left us but none of them stayed around for any great length of time and I was crushed at her missed opportunities to find companionship not just for herself but the entire family. I miss a father figure around the house who could dispense some sense of normality and discipline not just for us girls but mom as well. By mid afternoon I suggest Colleen get her clothes and we be on our way.

I told mom I would have her back the morning before they left and left her the phone number where to reach us and address as well. The short ride North up the five would take up fifteen minutes or so. Colleen conversed with the kids on our way home and they appeared to enjoy her company. They asked her all kinds of questions about what she was taking in school, her likes and hobbies and if she played ball like me. Such inquisitive questions for little kids I was amazed that they had that vocabulary to start! Renee went to school as well but just Kindergarten and Boyd stayed with an Aunt while we were at work.

I showed Colleen to our room and then the kids took her on a brief tour of the house and backyard. They spent most of their week-ends in their parent's bedroom while I had been occupying their bedroom but this would only last another month or so. I would inform Colleen that I had decided to return home and go to school. I expressed my interest in a number of fields from secondary school teacher, counselor or a writer maybe working with underprivileged, troubled children. The point was I would come home in a limited capacity because of my educational pursuit and nothing permanent.

I don't want her thinking that I'm going to bully my way back in the good graces of mom and bump her from her pedestal. Little did she know or believe that I was ever in mothers graces to say the least. It was imperative to me that she understand I have no ulterior motive in moving back home. She is fifteen and I have never been a threat to here it was always some self absorbed notion that I meant more to mom then any of them. Little did she know that I was the least important of the girls but most self sufficient and reliable then any of her other children. I was the fifth born and always carried the heaviest burdens.

I have no complaints. It's not something I ever thought about in that context. I did it out of instinct and the lessons of my grandmother. Her instructions were very exact and to the point. I was little but mature in an odd sense of the word. Having four older siblings who were lost in their own worlds by the time our parents divorced made life unbearable for a person like me. The people who were a nurturing force in my life died when I was ten and thirteen so by the time anything important came along, I was already well versed on the degradation of the American family. Divorce and permanent departure plucked any hope I had of reconciliation with self.

Kristopher was my soul mate and Grandmother my umbilical cord to God my Father. Their love and influence in my life is infinite and I have suffered their loss far deeper then anyone else in the family I know. My grieving is a life long process without closure. I am teetering on the edge of purgatory and ultimately am the only one who can make the decision whether to stay or let go. I am constantly looking for signs of inspiration and cultivation of peace in a shattered home life. My hope lays in the hands of a stranger whom can possible help me to save myself.

Colleen was pretty silent through most of the information I revealed to her about returning home but she made no objections nor offered any negative comments so I felt confident this would be alright at least at the beginning. I made no promises except to help mom however I could with what little money I brought home with me. It was made perfectly clear thought that I would be sharing the room with mom as here and Michelle occupied the second bedroom and was already crowded with furniture and book cases. I was not attempting to infringe or impose on their space as I made myself perfectly clear to her on that point.

It was a comforting visit and the children really enjoyed her company. They asked her if she would come back sometime again for another and she replied with an ear to ear smile "*YES*"! We lounged on the couch late into the evening before stumbling off to bed where we would return her to mom the next day and they would be off headed back to Oceanside and prepare for their first day of school the next day. I think Michelle enjoyed her separations from Colleen whenever they came about due to the comments she made to me previously about how mean Colleen could be to her at times.

They are very different in comparison to me where Colleen is somewhat selfish, over protective of her personal belongings and doesn't share well but I on the other hand am free spirited. What's mine is yours and use it as long as you need. My only stipulation is, take care of it if you want to borrow it in the future. I don't have much but am extremely sentiment of what I do have. I learned early on that you own nothing in this life and when your time comes you go out as you came in, with nothing as you cannot take anything with you. I came into this world naked and innocent without sin yet will perish scarred with blemishes and sin.

If there is any relationship I have to without a doubt mend, is that with God my Father. When I get depressed and drink or am consumed with anger and drink, I am not conscious of He who created me. I commence to churning all my emotional baggage and short comings with Him which usually results in fits of rage and disappointing one way conversation. I know God has been present in my life every solitary day of it but it has not been without disappointment. I have misunderstood on many occasions the friends I have acquired who have offered to give me emotional support.

There is a dark side of me that I must keep contained if I want to remain a free spirit. Enrolling in school will help me channel most of that unsavory energy into something meaningful and positive. Education has always been a cure for what ales me. I have spent my life in recovery and not doing very well with the battle. What's worse is that I am so much stronger, a true optimist and lover of all humanity, especially the four legged variety but don't always show it. My suit of armor is thick and very heavy with suspicions which therefore prevent me from behaving in a way that is true to my nature.

With life returning to normal once again and September moving along without further incident I take a walk back over to Tracy's house to inform her I have decided to move back home the end of October. I didn't see anything developing with her at her age and it was unfathomable that I could think otherwise with anyone her age. When the time game that I was ready enough to expose my reality it would only be when I was with a more mature woman preferably older then me. She seemed upset and disappointed and asked me if I would take her to my home some week-end to meet my family.

It was a request that not only shocked me but made me curious as to what her intentions were. I have no expectations of this girl but was willing, provided I had her parent's permission and left the necessary personal information as to where to reach her and my home address could I even consider taking her home. Tracy is the same age as Colleen and I didn't think about what my family might think I just asked mom if would be alright and she said only if she could speak to her parents directly. We let the mothers make the arrangements and if they agreed then I would take her with me my next trip and the end of the month.

I would furnish her the roundtrip bus ticket and we would leave mid morning and arrive by noon. I requested mom to be there when we arrived if at all possible because I didn't want to have to walk home from the station with a new, younger friend. Mom agreed and sounded sincere but I would have to see once we pulled around the corner off Hill Street. I told Luisa and the family of my intentions which brought a group of sad expressions. Renee and Boyd spoke up and asked why as I explained briefly that I wanted to go back to school and get my teaching credentials.

I really hadn't made up my mind yet as to which direction I was headed but that was a strong first and they could understand the importance of a teacher. Renee bragged about how nice her teacher was and gave her compliments often so maybe she could relate. I wanted to be a teacher so I could spend my days with wonderful children such as themselves. It sounded like such a wonderful thing I could believe it myself if I wasn't careful. When the end of September came around I informed my boss Chuck that I would be leaving sometime at the end of October.

His reaction wasn't negative one way or the other but inquired why just the same. I told him I was returning to school to get my teaching credentials. I figured that was a far more important occupation then spending my life at a job like this. I couldn't express my true feelings about how meaningless I felt doing this job and that God must have a better purpose for me then to spend my days doing this stuff. He had a meeting the next morning and told everybody I was leaving within the month. I would be going home this week end to talk to mom and bring Tracy with me. I wasn't anticipating the news to be unexpected as I'm sure she always felt that my leaving was only temporary to begin with.

I would explore the want ads to see what the job market was and take my first week home to visit Mira Costa Community College to check out their curriculum and schedule. I believe I am too late to enroll for this semester but I will be okay for the next. My co workers were both saddened and glad for me that I was getting out of this type of job. They felt I should have a pretty good chance to attain any option I wanted so long as I stayed with it. I would give them a definite date when I returned on Monday. There was a guy there who had asked me out on several occasions but I had always turned him down.

He was very good looking Porto Rican with the greenest eyes which always stimulated me beyond emotion but I never told him that. I couldn't bring myself to date a guy no matter how handsome and sweet they were. I am who I am and it wouldn't be right that when the time came that they wanted to get serious or wanted more then I was willing to give I would have to hurt them intentionally because I know the truth. I just couldn't inflict that kind of pain on another humane being. I wouldn't want someone to do that to me and I wasn't strong enough to flat out tell him I was not an ordinary girl.

I told him I was moving back home to pursue an education and get my teaching credentials. He seemed very sad at this news and asked if he could have my phone number so that he could keep in touch with me. We talked often enough here at work on breaks and at lunch when sometimes we would go for walks off the site. He is a light skinned African American with deeply moving eyes, green at that! Because I didn't want to hurt his feelings and our relationship was completely innocent I gave him my phone number at moms and never actually expected him to call.

If I was any other type of girl I might have given him a chance but I knew better. The week-end was here and our trip back home was upon us. Tracy's mother dropped us off at the depot in West Hollywood where we would transfer to a bus when we arrived in Los Angeles. There was so much going on in my head that I wasn't sure if I could pay attention to anything Tracy was saying once we reached our seats. She kindly acknowledged her gratitude for my paying for her ticket. We started out talking about what it was like at her High School and some of the traditions they followed.

Seems no matter where you live High Schools in general all have standard traditions of school spirit and community support. She is the typical teenager going through school taking the recommended curriculum littered with electives of her choice and a sport if she so chooses. I don't see myself so much as a mentor as I do a good friend. She's always wanted to come south and see the San Diego area although I explained my location in comparison to San Diego. Oceanside is approximately forty or so miles North of San Diego but you can get there anywhere from thirty to forty five minutes depending on traffic.

Although our traffic down here is not to be compared to Los Angeles traffic with all the hustle and bustle of people and mass transit. I didn't offer much personal information about myself or family directly but I did inform her about Colleen and Michelle, their ages and briefly about our relationship as sisters. I told her my parents were divorced since I was ten and that mom still dates but dad was remarried. I was very skeptical about any family details or history since our relationship was in transformation. I didn't expect to hear from her again once I moved back home.

By the time we reached the off ramp for the bus depot and turned into the station she had lots of questions already. I explained where the beach was from there and we could walk there from, the station and look around. I pointed out to the empty lot where there used to be a go cart track back in the day and a block of Arcades which are now empty buildings. It is said for me to reflect upon the recent past when Oceanside was so much more of a family based town of military personnel and regular folk. I truly missed those days but at least we still had the roller rink.

By the time we stepped off the bus I could see Michelle and Colleen standing off to the side waving at me. We gathered our little belongings and headed toward them and the car. I made the formal introductions and the girls were cordial. Mom had driven down in her Lemans which she still has had fixed from that minor traffic incident during Matthews graduation two years ago. I suppose it really made no difference to her since the car was still drivable and it didn't affect her entrance or exit from the car. But if it was my car, I would have had it fixed as soon as I could when I had the money.

Since I wasn't aware of any plans mom might have arranged I didn't want to offer the suggestion of going to the zoo but did suggest we see a movie. I would bring up other excursions later in the evening when mom and I are alone. She seemed closer to Colleen then Michelle or I and that was good. I didn't want anybody to get the wrong impression or draw untrue conclusions. When they got themselves preoccupied in their room I asked mom if we could talk a bit. She looked reluctant at first but said "*alright*". I expressed my wishes to coming back home but in a limited role because I was planning on attending school and getting my teaching credentials.

Home would be more like a place for me to rest my head and study, not that I would have any say or responsibility for anything that went on there. I was essentially relinquishing my status for the sake of everybody getting along. I didn't want to disrupt the flow of how things were now. There was so much for me to say, secrets to share but it wasn't an appropriate time with Tracy here and all. I felt uncomfortable and afraid she would assume that Tracy and I was an item; nothing could be further from the truth. In conclusion to our informal conversation she agreed that my coming home would be alright and she saw no problem with either of the girls.

By the time I got back to the girls nobody wanted to go to the movies but instead wanted to go to the beach and walk around. That was just as well since mom would be able to drop us off and pick us up in a couple hours. She has a date and didn't want to worry about coming down to get us. All the same since we could walk home from there if we had to and it wasn't too late. I was glad the house was clean and I showed Tracy where she would be sleeping. She could take the couch and I would sleep in mom's room providing she wasn't bring her date home for the night. Matthew resided in the garage still and I hardly every saw much of him.

I thanked her for that consideration on this trip home. Colleen asked me how the kids, Renee and Boyd were doing and I replied *"just fine"*. I didn't want to be the bearer of sad news when I came home that Luisa and Thwat were having marital issues. It wasn't really anybody's business and I had confidence that they would work it out. They have two small children to think about and therefore someone was bound to make a compromise. I wasn't about to share the gossip I was privy to and felt more like it was just a passing obstacle they would overcome. I couldn't give up on them because of the children.

We gathered a few towels, got our flip flops and jumped in the car for the short trip to the beach. September is the beginning of the cooling trend and I knew that if we were going to be walking home that we had better get our shop looking done early and enjoy the scenery early as possible. It would take us about forty five minutes to an hour to reach the house from the harbor. We would have mom drop us off at the pier where we would start from there. I showed Tracy the shell where I had graduated and where Colleen will graduate in two years. She was in awe at the background it offered and wished she lived down here.

For the remainder of the day and early evening before the sun began to set we hung out around the beach with others littered up and down the coast for the last few weeks of beach weather. I skimmed the newspaper looking in the ads section to see what kinds of jobs were available in my field of manufacturing. I would write down the ones which interested me for future use when I returned home and thought I would call then. I would also check out Mira Costa College to see what courses they were offering and would make an appointment to see a counselor.

Mom had prepared some Mexican food for dinner and we made our own bean burritos with Spanish rice. I so missed her cooking and was glad to see that hadn't gone totally fast food. I had gotten used to Betty's out of this world cooking when I lived with them and shared meals with my other cousins who also lived on the same street but a few house up from theirs. Thwat and his brother in law did most of the cooking at the house simply because it's their culture to cook while the women attended other duties of the household. It wasn't that Luisa or her sister couldn't cook because when the men were out playing basket ball or what have you, girls ruled the kitchen.

I may have assisted the cooks in the kitchen wherever I lived but I never was the primary cook who prepared and served a meal on my own. I would cook for mom and the girls but nobody else. By the end of our visit when Sunday came around and we cleaned up after our showers and got ready to return I told mom I would be back by then end of the month, I just couldn't give her a definite date. I would have Richard bring me down with my trunk and everything I owned packed inside. I had an idea but didn't want to say just in case something came up. Tracy said she had enjoyed herself even if we didn't make it to the zoo but loves the beach and thinks my sisters are nice.

The walk back was more silent then our trip down and I was thankful for that. I needed some rest and contemplated what answer I would give Chuck when I went in to work tomorrow. October is a long month and I really would like to stick around for Halloween and enjoy the surprises of little children dressed up in their favorite characters! It would take me back to the days I remember as a child and all the fun we use to have. I was so in awe of the lives of children and all the things they would say and do when they were around. I regretted not having one of my own.

Loneliness is a terrible thing and one emotion I try to avoid at any cost and circumstance. We called Tracy's mother once we pulled into the Los Angles station and told her what time our transfer bus would arrive in West Hollywood for her to meet us there. Both her mother and father are very nice people and her little brother was cool as well. A little wild and rambunctious at times but that's a little boy for you and I could definitely relate. I explained to her that I probably wouldn't be able to see her before I left and made sure she had my phone number. I told her I would keep in touch often as I could.

I gave Chuck two weeks notice and would leave the middle of October. In this time period I contacted my former companion through his job and told him I was moving back to Oceanside and would not have the opportunity to see him again. I didn't want him to call me at Luisa's house any longer or stop by. The woman at work who had flirted with me on so many occasions I let know that I was sorry I never took her up on any invitations to lunch, coffee or other rendezvous. As strongly as I felt I wanted to and curious as I was my inner child always intervened.

My cousins, Richard and Betty and the kids, Ed and Mary and their kids, Cecilia, Octovio and the kids whom I felt closest too along with Aunt Connie and Uncle Felix expressed mixed feelings about my returning home. They all have been inspirations is their own way to me and I will miss all the children the most. Their company, our parties and gatherings and all the things we did and places we went on week-ends sometimes have left me with the fondest of memories that I will cherish all the days of my life. I would not let them see me cry so I made my phone calls brief.

My last weeks at work were no less productive then any other week. I did piece work and enjoyed the tasks given me. Making the insides of thermostats wasn't the most fulfilling job but it was my first and I was thankful not only for the experience but the opportunity to meet and work with some very nice people. Most of the older women were friends of Aunt Connie whom was a symbol of kindness for others. She was a one woman welcoming committee. I would miss people like Millie Chandler whom had gifted me a very expensive pair of loop earrings and reminded me of my favorite actress; Susan Hayward.

They had set aside last break to celebrate my leaving, share a cake and wish me good luck sending me off with a gift of fifty dollars. They told me good luck in my pursuit of higher education and let them know when I graduated and became a teacher! I would miss them but not the work and hoped that I could pursue such goal without further interruptions or distractions. Thwat, Luisa and the kids would drive me back down in their friend's truck on Saturday morning. We had a small party at the house when we got home where Thwat, his brother in law and a few friends had already gathered and prepared a big meal for the occasion.

All the familiar smells and odors filled the house as I could hear children laughing in the background. I told Thwat in confidence that I would seriously consider his friends proposal to marry him and make the necessary arrangements for him to get his green card and eventually his citizenship. I felt bad that I didn't just pursue that avenue and collect the ten grand but I was uncertain to all the details and expectations that were involved. It would remain a thought at least for now. The party stated as soon as I changed my clothes and joined the others. There was a full sheet cake on the dinning room table that read GOOD LUCK MIRACLE.

I felt I had a purpose now and I didn't want to disappoint anybody so when I got home I would get in touch with Mira Costa first thing and make an appointment to see a counselor. It is my understanding that as long as I was going to school full time and living at home I would be able to collect unemployment. We stayed up pretty late visiting, playing cards, games and celebrating until well past midnight when the kids had fallen asleep on the couch or various visitors' laps. This congregation of so many people reminded me of past family celebrations when I was Renee and Boyd's age.

I didn't drink because I had a busy day tomorrow and I wanted to be in my right mind without a pounding headache. I had nearly five hundred dollars saved which included my last check and the money I received as presents but I would not take out or close my credit union account I had through ITT. As long as I remained paying my dues I could keep my money in there until such a time when I transferred it to my own account down in Oceanside. I liked my independence and hoped I didn't lose too much of it upon my return to the family. I told mom I would continue to share my funds with her as I was able but keep some for myself so I could buy a car.

It was my intention to move back temporarily for as long as I could stand it without creating any discord. By the time the last guests left it was well after midnight. The kitchen had already been cleaned up and trash taken out. It was amazing to me how in sync these people work when other's a lot of food and the kitchen is hopping the whole time. Between the huge pots of two different types of curries, noodles, barbecues and numerous varieties of drinks, there was no food dropped, anything spilled or droppings left upon the stove. They are impeccably organized cooks in that kitchen no matter how big the party! I was impressed to say the least.

We were on the road by nine o'clock to beat the traffic as the kids jumped in the back of the truck with me once we lifted the truck in the back of the truck. It was a bit nippy out and the sun was already moving upward from the east over the mountains which I loved. I would miss everything about this area and landscape but know that at any time I could return since there was an open invitation. I sat between both kids as they laid their heads upon my lap once we pulled away from the curb. I had called mom to tell her we were leaving and would arrive in about two to two and a half hours.

LIVE OR DIE

I felt sad inside that I had failed to stay up here and make a go of life on my own. I should have pursued a junior college up here and done the same things here as I was promising to do down there. I didn't have the strength or assertiveness to be my own person no matter how much I wanted to. I was disappointed in myself for being to weak and allowing my inner child to have such influence over any decisions I made. I am going to be nineteen in three months and hope to God I will have a plan to move out on my own or with someone else. I cannot allow myself to get sucked back in to a nonproductive environment.

I tried to think of nothing on the ride home as Luisa and Thwat asked me inquiring questions about Oceanside and what was there main industry. I had been away for a year now and had no idea what the industry was since my interest was to begin school and pursue my teaching credentials or counseling degree. I wasn't afraid of anything except ending up in a rut of going to school without having a clear purpose and settling for a no brainer assembly job. Education is important to me because it allows you to have some measure of power when you learn things and then apply them to a job you train for.

I see so many young people who take education for granted, are lazy and waste their time bumming around the beach or the street. That is such a waste of one's mind. I say that if you're bored in school or don't know what you want in life, join the military and get an education where you will learn something of interest to you. Only you can determine what your dreams and goals are not your parents or friends. I love school and the pursuit of happiness in my job but my first priority is getting myself organized. I still intend having that; mom I'm a lesbian conversation but I need to be more responsible and address it at the appropriate time.

My foremost dilemma and crisis is not directly with mom and my siblings but with God. I know to well what is said in the Bible under any version and I know how society feels about people like me. I am only one person and cannot stand up to an entire nation alone. I am not a Dr. Martin Luther King Jr. My education has been through the experiences of life itself without the support of an educational institutional system. There is no text book in the world that addresses the issues of being gay. There are lots of suppositions and recommendations for cures for people afflicted with what they determine is more a disease and social condition then a fact of life.

My battles I'm afraid have not yet begun and if I am going to begin a life that is fulfilling to me, if I am going to realize my purpose in this world it will have to be through the support of someone with more education then family, friends and society as a whole. Aside from contacting the local colleges to set up an appointment for a counselor I will give the families' therapist a call and make arrangements to see her as well on Colleens next visit if it's acceptable. I know mom sees her on occasion as well so this whole adventure should be quite interesting. I look forward to her opinion of the situation.

We made it all the way home without stopping for gas, food or to use a bathroom. The children slept on my lap the entire way. The ocean was crystal clear and you could see a few scattered sailboats on the horizon as the sun reflected brightly off the water. There was not too much traffic and we had a pretty easy time of it. The kids awoke as soon as we pulled to the curb and Colleen and Michelle came out to greet us. They said mom had made a fresh pot of coffee and would cook some breakfast if anybody was hungry. Colleen collected the kids as they followed her and Luisa into the house. I helped Thwat take the trunk off of the truck and set it inside the garage.

Those who needed to relieve themselves headed for the bathroom as the rest went into the kitchen for something to drink. Mom offered Luisa a cup of coffee and poured one half full for Thwat. I offered to scramble some eggs and bacon and Colleen would roll out the tortilla dough that mom had prepared ahead of time earlier that morning. The kids sat with Colleen at the table while I took over duties of cooking the tortillas. I liked how the kids enjoyed Colleen's company so fast when they hadn't really known her as long as they have me. I guess it's all good if you stop and think about it. Their happy and that's all that matters.

They stayed long enough to rest up, have a bite to eat and then mom sent them home with containers of food just in case they got hungry on the way home. Mom and Luisa spoke amongst themselves when Thwat gathered up the kids and headed for the truck. I tried to offer him a twenty dollar bill to help for gas in appreciation for them driving me down but he wouldn't take it. He wrapped his long arms around my round body and hugged me tight expressing his thanks for living with them as long as I did and helping out with the kids. I was a fun source of entertainment for everybody in the house.

I bent over to lift the kids up for one last hug and set them inside the cab of the truck. I hugged Luisa next and told her I would certainly keep in touch and for them to call me anytime they need my services for anything and I emphasized *anything.* We waved to the kids as they pulled away and drove to the end of the street to make a u-turn and head back towards the freeway. When they were out of sight I headed back in the house and went to help clean the kitchen. I wasn't sure how I felt about being home. I needed to assess the situation a little further which I really couldn't do until I took care of my errands this week.

There was no need to unpack since the only thing of any importance was my clothes which needed either to be washed or put away. Mom had emptied one of her dresser for me to put my clothes in until I was able to get my own. I expressed to her that I would sleep on the couch when the time came that she would be having her dates stay over. She nodded her head in agreement and nothing further was spoken about the subject. It would be a mission of mine to get my life organized and look for someone to share an apartment with. I did not feel comfortable.

Come Monday the girls had returned to school and mom went to work. She told me I could use her car if I needed when it was time to go over to Mira Costa. I told her I would also look for a job as well. I asked Colleen to inquire of her therapist if I could meet with her on her next appointment this week and she said yes. There was so much to do and I was anxious to get some answers. I could not afford to be idle for any period of time so the sooner I got moving the faster I can get on with my life. I had also hoped to find being home a means for losing some of the weight I picked up through my months of drinking and other bad habits.

I was not happy carrying this extra weight and would do whatever it took to discard it. I have always been active in sports and something else I wanted to do was call Mrs. Moore to see if I could rejoin the team. I missed playing ball this past year and knew it would easy for me to get in shape. By then end of October I had gathered all the information on my list of things to do. I would attend night school next semester and would sign up for the classes my counselor advised. Mrs. Moore said I could come back and I went to see her to get a schedule and visit a while.

I would meet Colleen's therapist after one of her visits in November. I decided to join *Writers Book* club and *Psychology Today* and get a little background on how to deal with indifferent children whether it be psychological, physical or mental' I wanted to be aware of anything that was possible and that covers a lot of ground. I needed to go back to Mira Costa for some testing to see where I was at scholastically and what not, my strengths and weaknesses and then determine my next plan of action from there. What field best suited me. I would read the daily newspaper to see what jobs were available in the area and call any I felt I might qualify for.

I would hold off once again talking to mom about my coming out until after the visit with the therapist. I wanted an outside opinion of what I could expect and hopefully a little support on how to respond since we basically have no relationship and never did. I would hope she would be objective. It is a field of great interest for me as well that perhaps I might want to pursue in counseling adolescents that have suffered as I did. There is a heavy burden to share and I have to feel comfortable enough to open this wound to a total stranger. It's a step I have no choice but to take if I'm going to continue living.

I know what happens when I get depressed and I am unable to escape its grip. That island of exile I retreat to when I have lost all tolerance for the ignorance and insensitive people of this world. I seldom see compassionate acts of kindness from others just for the sake of it. I am not out to hurt or bring shame to my parents or family members. My being lesbian is not a result of being sexually abused and hounded by male relatives as a child. As told by my grandmother and knowing this to be true according to what she taught me; that only God has the seeds which have been planted in the womb of a woman who bares a child in the image that God has chosen. Each seed is unique and one of a kind.

I am not a religious scholar by any means nor have I studied extensively any of the religions of the world but I do know the love of my Father. Nobody knows the relationship that He and I have shared all of my life. The only one to pass judgment over me is my Father and I will answer to Him accordingly. This is an issue I will stand up for under any circumstances. I don't know of any person whom can compare themselves to the likeness and works of God. I learned very early on that God is my armor and I cannot be destroyed. Now people will attempt to do me harm physically but they will not reach that which God protects. My heart is His dwelling place let no one mistake this.

When I am surrounded by a great debate within myself I seek the readings of my Fathers good book. He has known about me from the moment I was extracted from my mother's womb. What I choose to do with this knowledge is up to me. I exist to do the work of my Father. I want to be a rest stop on the road for others who are searching for acceptance and support. I choose to follow in the footsteps of my Father who shows endless acts of mercy and empathy for all mankind. I admire and respect the traditions and cultures of the American Indian whom holds undeniable respect for mother earth and all its inhabitants.

I am not schooled in the way of politics and religions but I do know that in these uncertain times that many have strayed from the path of mercy and kindness. The best way I know how to stand besides my Father is to continue to show endless acts of kindness by my faith not just by saying my faith will carry me through. I know the sin of suicide and it's consequences but my Father is merciful and I would be forgiven. One cannot take their own life if it has already been lost by the acts of another. It has been a lifelong struggle and I have had to force myself to want to live. Question is, do I live or die? Nothing in life fascinates me yet everything about death enchants me.

A person can only absorb so much distress and discontentment before they give in. I have needed all my years of adolescence the opportunity to tell someone. My behavior in the past with certain individuals costed me not only their friendship but a lifetime source of understanding and support. I regret the indescribable agony I caused them and will never be forgiven by them or myself. I am not one to fear death but quite the opposite, fearing life on a daily basis. It is lonely when you have nobody in which to communicate with. I continually talk to my Father but I cannot hear His replies.

I do not expect compassion from any religious institution because I am deemed a sinner. The church does not dispense compassion or mercy for those who do not walk as they do. Being gay is an abomination not just against God but the Church and all of mankind. I have heard this sermon on every religious radio station on the air. I see how others are repulsed by the admission of being lesbian. I may never be able to live under the same roof with my mother and tell her the truth. Yet I can no longer continue to pretend being the daughter she thinks I am. The burden of truth is a much heavier cross then I can carry.

With November upon us, Matthew and Kris's birthday and Thanksgiving holiday nearing there is some sad news. Aunt Connie has called to inform us that Uncle Felix has passed away. There is a feeling of shock and sadness that hovers over me. He and I had managed to mend what we could of our quilted past. I had forgiven him his faults of the past but never quite found closure. We had learned to be friends in an odd sense of the way. He was my Uncle and I loved him because it was how we were raised. It was a strict Catholic upbringing to love, obey and respect your elders. Honor your Mother and Father and so on and so forth.

These are lessons branded not only in my mind but heart as well. Grandmothers are the umbilical cords of life with God and whatever it is they say children automatically file it in both their minds and hearts as the ultimate truth next to God himself. The things which occurred between Uncle Felix and me cannot be repaired but I have learned to have mercy and forgiveness for him because he changed, he stopped. The times we spent together this past year was filled with meeting his other friends and wanting to be sure that I understood he was not the same man from my earlier years.

The funeral arrangements were being attended to and it would be within the week. I could not cry at first because now I felt completely safe. I felt safe for my sisters whom could have been but I diverted his attention from them to me instead. I couldn't image them suffering as I do. I will say a prayer for him tonight and share my thoughts and feelings about him. I will surely miss him for there were times of great adventures with him and other family events. Mom told the girls that he had passed away but did not suffer any pain. They did not know him as I had and thus spared from certain truths. I have a bittersweet mercy for him.

The weather's been chilly lately and we will need to dress warm for the service. The girls have been excused from school, Matthew took off from work and we will be up in Glendale in support of the loss that has occurred. I know how sad his grandchildren must feel right now because they were all very close to him. They are an extraordinarily close family. I like that they all live on the same street Linden; from the first corner house where Richard, Betty and the kids reside up a few houses where Eddie, Mary and their three kids live, next door where Cecilia, Octovio and their three kids and then several houses further up are Aunt Connie and Uncle Felix.

I hungered for a family of my own to be that close. I wasn't sure how to react when I saw Aunt Connie and the rest of the family. I had just settled in from returning home and now I am back to show respect to a man who brought such controversy to my life. I hated him for what he did but learned to find a way to forgive. He is no longer a threat but still I shall miss him. His favorite thing was for me, any of us kids to massage his scalp when we would come up for visits. Our reward was all the change he had in his pockets. That was the prize but in the end I don't know who was most excited. I will miss him none the less.

The church was filled with so many people, some I recognized because they are family and others nearer the back of the church I didn't recognize. I followed mom to the front near the rest of the family where the usher had directed us to take our seats in the pew behind her and the kids. I kissed her out of respect without comment as she said; "*I had meant a lot to him*". Our secret could never be revealed and so it shall be buried with him for all eternity. I must decide right then whether or not I want to say goodbye as others who pay their last respects at his open coffin.

The service went on it seems forever as I vaguely heard others whimper and sniffle. I held my sisters hands as they sat either side of me. I reflected upon my memories of him and the more fun times we had with family on visits to the house, the beach or parks. The longer I remained seated in that pew behind Aunt

Connie and the rest of the family the darker my surroundings felt. There was a deep sense of loss creeping into my thoughts and I just wanted the Priest to hurry up. I took my place in line behind the others when it was time to leave and the service had been concluded. Walking behind the coffin I prayed silently that God have mercy on his soul.

I had been unable to eat the day or two before we came up since we got the call. My appetite is ruled by my emotional state of mind. Perhaps if I remained in this sullen mood for a few weeks longer I could get back down to the weight I was use to. The boys had taken their places beside the casket to the steps of the church which then would be taken to the hearse that waited down below on the street. I thought back to this same event five years earlier when Kristopher had died and we suffered this same chain of events. I was five years younger but to me it was in that same moment when I could visualize Kris's service all over again.

Like grandmother, his loss has never healed and the emptiness I still feel drowns me in melancholy. When the family has been ushered into their vehicles for the procession to the cemetery and we gather in line behind them it is an eerie feeling to be going through this experience so soon. It was not that long ago that I saw him and the family. He was not sick or had been feeling poorly that I was aware of yet in a blink of an eye he had perished. Thank God Aunt Connie was with him at the time and I will be sure to get the details later when it's less hectic. I had never known that regular people could be buried at Forrest Lawn.

I thought it was for the rich and famous! It was larger then my eyes could see and there were miles of cars behind ours. There were so many people here that I could not see the cars any longer. Of course they are mostly adults as us kids are herded towards the front with their parents or sitting on their laps. After people have finished clearing their throats, blowing their noses and other idle noises are silenced the Priest begins the prayer. It is a bright sunny day with a slight chill in the air. I look around at others in my view and try to image how they must feel. This is their grandfather about to be set down six feet beneath this plush green grass.

I had wished to have shared this same privilege when my grandmother passed away and none of us children were allowed to attend her service. I thought it quite cruel that I of all her younger grandchildren was denied access to the service for reasons I've never known, not even to this day. There has been no closure for me concerning her and I have carried this resentment all my life. While I stood here thinking about times long past the Priest has come over to Aunt Connie, the kids and his mother and father expressing his condolences. People have come over to express their condolences and place their flowers upon his casket prior to being lowered beneath the ground.

This is not how I intend on taking my journey to my Father's house when the time comes. I want to be cremated and even have it down in writing with date and signature for when that time ever comes and I can no longer take any more. Everything is in its place and instructions will be known by more then just my mother. I placed my hand upon his casket and bit him farewell for I knew that one day I would see him again. I did not shed one solitary tear yet wept in silence for his loss. We followed others back to Linden where we would be joining others in celebration of his life. I would stay close to the girls while Matthew went looking for our cousins more his age.

I waited a long while before I approached his mother and father to give my condolences and kiss their cheeks. I loved his parents, mostly because they were surrogate grandparents for me even thought I didn't get to see them as often as I would have liked. I needed grandparents because since grandmother died my tree of wisdom had gone dormant and I had nobody to dispense any worthwhile lessons on the rules of life. My mentor and teacher had gone and left me with no substitute. I know that grandparents are irreplaceable but there should be a proxy among the family.

We remained here staying at various homes of my cousins until Sunday when we made our journey back home. In spite of the circumstances it was nice being with all my little cousins again. I promised them we would be back for Thanksgiving and continue our little games. I have missed them and began to wonder if I didn't make a mistake going back. I could have very well stayed up here and done the same things. I've never been very good at making the right choices or decisions. I enjoyed what time I could spend with the girls of the family, Cecilia, Betty and others. Matthew enjoyed the company of the boys as well.

I told them I would spend much more time helping them at Thanksgiving when we returned for the family gathering this year under the circumstances. I've always preferred holidays up here in Glendale because the boys, the girls as well for any who wanted to join in would walk up to the observatory where we played football in the park. It was only a few blocks from the house at that time but now that they reside on Linden I'm not sure what we'll be doing this year. Family sports has always been a big attraction for us and more fun then I had since childhood with them when we use to all meet at the beach in Carlsbad.

Nobody had much to say on the drive back home. Mom did mention the events that lead up to his death though. He had gone to the hospital because he wasn't feeling well and then one thing lead to another and all this time Aunt

Connie had been with him up until the time he sat up and smiled reaching out for someone and then lay back down and passed away.

I wasn't sure if I heard the details clearly but I thought what a wonderful way to go if you seem to see something nobody else in the room sees and peace is upon you then next thing you know you're on your way.

My last wishes to be cremated will remain. I cannot stand the thought of being entombed in the ground or any other place for that matter, like it says in the Bible ashes to ashes dust to dust. We came from dust and so shall we return as dust. Or perhaps like the Buddhist believes in reincarnation, I just will not allow anyone the right to bury me in any enclosure. I offered to give mom some money for gas and she replied that only if she needed it. I told her I would participate in any helping out or cooking they might need for Thanksgiving. She said they would let us know what to bring up.

I had been doing some reading lately on autistic children and find some fascinating information within the covers of these books. There are six in the series and I have to budget myself as not to spend all my money on books and magazines. I had lost nearly fifteen pounds since I returned and my eating habits were very sporadic. I hadn't really tried to contact any school buddies to tell them I had come back since I figured I run into them sooner or later. The same people were still on the softball team but we all were getting older and within the next two years or so would have to move on to the next level whatever that was.

I was looking forward to rejoining the team and having some real fun. Nobody had really heard from Kammillie and the kids in a while so we couldn't inform her of the death of Uncle Felix. It probably wouldn't matter to her one way or the other anyhow since she had been out of touch with the family for so long. The girls went back to school as did mom back to work until Thanksgiving was upon us. I had asked Michelle if she had Mrs. Snyder for her P.E teacher this semester and she said yes but that she didn't like her! I'm beginning to wonder if Michelle isn't the real rebel in the family!

Michelle is a smart girl but is easily bullied no thanks to Colleen. More then once already she has come home complaining about the girls who are picking on her. I have it in my mind to follow her home from school one day just to see for myself but then I need to give her some time. It's a new school and people are different so she may just need to adjust to different attitudes and behaviors. I never had these problems in school because I knew mostly everybody including the tough Samoan girls and people knew better then to mess with the Samoans because they wouldn't think twice about kicking your but no questions asked.

I fit right in because a lot of people had heard about me and my reputation as well as found out about both while participating in P.E. class. I was friendly with most of the eighth graders already having played softball outside of school with them. We would start practice with Mrs. Moore's team after we returned from Thanksgiving holiday. I wasn't ready to join them for their tournament but gladly when I got back. I don't know where all the time has gone since I got back. We were to bring side dishes and a dessert. Naturally our dessert was pumpkin pies that mom made since they were our favorite. We brought a big bowl of mashed potatoes and cranberry sauce in the can, six.

The weather had started to turn a bit chilly so we packed sweaters and long pants. We were invited to stay at various houses and I elected to stay with Cecilia and her family while Michelle and Colleen stayed with mom. Aunt Stella and couple of the kids came up, Aunt Josephine and Uncle Manuel and Karla came as did a few others from down south. It was a good time to be together. For the next few hours I helped when they needed me while the younger kids played at various houses with their cousins. The neighborhood was littered with family up and down the street. Matthew could be found cavorting with Richard and Eddie as usual.

This holiday has to be my favorite one along with Christmas because of the joy and happiness you see on a child's face. The holiday went along with out incident as family spent the evening enjoying the festivities of the meal and one another's company. There was much to talk about among the adults while us first cousins huddled in the living room and talked girl talk while the men were out doing men stuff whatever that might have been. There was plenty of food leftover for the following days and now there was a period of digestion before coffee and dessert was served.

The girls proceeded to ask me if I was working and when I replied no I went on to explain that I would start school this coming semester and probably look for a job depending on how my testing went. If I carry a full load I will be collecting unemployment but if not I will have to get a job. I expressed my choices of becoming a secondary school teacher or juvenile counselor. Either way I would be working with children which are what I truly dreamt of doing when I grew up given the opportunity. I went further by telling them how much I missed them and the kids and that I hoped I hadn't made a mistake by moving back home.

They exchanged looks between one another but said nothing, only those looks! Evening moved along as people began packing up to go to their prospective homes and get their children to bed. Mom would be staying here with Aunt Connie, Aunt Josephine and Uncle Manuel stayed as well and Karla came down with me and Cecilia. The girls went with Richard and Betty and their kids. It was a bit crowded but slumber parties are always fun, especially when family is involved! We hung around and talked another hour or so after the kids went to sleep then we headed for our prospective sleeping arrangements ourselves. Matthew also stayed over at Richard's.

Karla had inquired when the last time I had seen or heard from Kammillie was and I told her it had been quite a while. I didn't care for her to much lately so I wasn't really missing her compared to mom. There was always a wedge between us and it had only thickened over time so she wasn't much use to me. I liked hanging around Karla because we did some crazy things like drive around exclusive neighborhoods on trash day and rummage through their "junk" with our lights off of course just like I use to with Cecilia and Octovio in the days before their children came along.

The remainder of the week end was spent hanging out around the house catching up and talking about the things each of the kids were up to. It was ironic how our cousins up here each have three children, two boys and one girl. Talk about miracles! They are all pretty close in age but Danny is the youngest of Cecile's, Michelle the youngest of Ed's and Lacy the youngest of Richard and Betty. I believe that we and Uncle Robert and Aunt Mela have the most children, seven each. With Thanksgiving coming to an end and life having to move on everybody heads back to their homes and I tell my cousins I will hopefully be up here for Christmas.

I thought it might be a good idea to talk to mom and see what her plans were before I made any false promises to spend Christmas up there. Maybe Aunt Connie wants to travel down here or just spend it with her immediate family I can't say at this point. I will let mom find out the scoop as time goes by but for now we must get back the duties of everyday life.

The girls will get back to school and mom back to work while I continue with my home studying. There are a few jobs advertised in the paper that I will call this week and see if I can apply for them. It's nice that a couple of them are close to home.

With December here so has arrived the cold weather with it. I am anxious for my meeting with the therapist this afternoon after Colleen's session and looking forward to the experience. I have kept myself busy around the house and cleaning out the garage and tried what I could to get the backyard cleaned up a bit. I hated a dirt yard with no grass. I decided to give Carl a call and let him know I was back at home again. I hadn't seen him since graduation and I missed his enormous sense of humor. I recollected the times back in high school when we were juniors before I started dating Mark when he let me use his old rambler to learn how to drive.

That was quite the fiasco in the beginning as I could not negotiate curbs or distance for stopping at stop signs and lights. It was a big boxy car that needs to be handled differently then an ordinary vehicle. You needed to make wide turns around corners less you end up and over each curb. There are only fond memories with him all through our lives. He was the first of our neighbors growing up that I tormented as a child. He's like a brother to me and will always remain a part of my life. I figured we'd see each other before the holidays and grab a bite to eat or take a drive down to the pier and talk.

These past couple of months has been eye opening for me in many respects. Mom is dating a guy nearer her age with two teenage children of his own. I would like nothing more then for her to marry this guy bit we'll just have to see how it goes. Colleen and Michelle go about their lives like ordinary teenagers. They have their own interests and friends they congregate with which keeps them preoccupied from one another. Mom remains the same by working at the Head Start program at Balderamma Park with Aunt Stella who is the director and her other friend Clara. They have been friends many years now. Matthew continues to trudge along with his life as well.

Having received the results of my testing it has been determined that I favor the field of counseling first and perhaps teaching second. It made no difference to me since my objective is to work with children in any capacity. Unemployment denied me because I would not be carrying a full load at school. Therefore I would be seeking a job as soon as possible and attend classes at night. I know mom will allow me use of the car as long as I paid for the gas. I was a bit nervous about meeting the therapist because I wasn't sure what questions to ask first. I have multitudes of inquiries about so many issues, where does one start?

It is mid December and we are not going north for Christmas. All is well as it might be best they spend some time alone this first Christmas without Uncle Felix. They certainly are welcome at anyone's houses down this way and would most likely be down afterwards. We would be spending the week sending out Christmas cards as well which is what my task is after I return home from my visit. I waited anxiously in the office looking around at the pictures on the wall and magazines on the shelves and table in front of me. Mom also see's her when she's having a hard time of things but not as often as Colleen.

I asked Colleen to go ahead and give mom a call to come pick us up because this wasn't an actual hour long session but just an introduction to see if I feel comfortable enough around her to share. Her name is Pamela and she greets me with a warm smile and a hello, nice to meet you. I extended my hand to shake hers as she said good afternoon to Colleen and she reached to open the door so we could make our exit down the three steps towards her office. I was feeling pretty excited and wanting to share a few things immediately but kept my patience. She told me I had a very pretty name and was curious of its origin and was there a story.

I explained the situation of how I was the fourth child born on the sixteenth of a month, not the same month however just the date was the same and that all three of my brothers share the same birth date as me. Our oldest sister Kammillie actually ruined it by coming out on the sixth! Her office is small with lots of wall stuff and bookcases filled with all sorts of books and trinkets. She was the same height as me with long wavy dark hair and such a sweet voice. She didn't walk straight up with her shoulders squared the way I do and I wondered if she had some ailment that caused her to have a slight slump to her posture.

I couldn't dare ask her because this was our first meeting and there was no significance to the question. I have more pertinent questions to ask of her. She asked what it was like returning home after nearly a year. I told her things were going alright and there were no earth shattering drama going on, no conflicts nor jealousy expressed. I asked her how I go about coming to see her once or twice a month to start until we determine if this was sufficient. She asked me why I was seeking the services of a therapist and I explained. I skirted around the truth to start by telling her I wanted to become a counselor for neglected, troubled kids and just wanted to be assed by a professional.

I had to be sure my past history wouldn't cloud my judgments or have any ill effects on the children. What I was essentially asking for was a clean bill of mental health before I moved in to this field to deep. I told her that she must know by now our family history in that we had spent many months in therapy as a family when we were teenagers after our dad left us. I knew she was also seeing mom and that surely she has some opinion about the situation. First she told me I could apply for assistance to be covered for my medical needs and then I could set up a schedule to meet with her until I got a job.

I was thankful Colleen was her last patient for the day and I wouldn't have to feel so rushed but I knew at the conclusion of our meeting I definitely wanted to return. I felt there was hope I could trust her enough to share my deepest, darkest secrets without being condemned or looked upon negatively. I expressed my willingness to discuss some more personal issues after we've gotten past the initial introductions to the rules and expectations of this whole therapy thing. She assured me there were no rules or expectations and only I as the patient could determine my own expectations from these sessions.

We walked back to the office together as I noticed mom parked along the curb at the end of their front lawn. I told her I would make the necessary arrangements and take care of any paperwork I needed to get started and see her soon. I told her how nice it was to finally meet her and looked forward to our next discussion. I was now quite convinced that she was the one as I walked over to the car behind Colleen. Michelle was in the back seat and I figured there was some place for us to go. Mom asked what I thought of her and I said I thought she was very nice and I found it easy to speak to her.

I wasn't seeing her as a patient so to speak right then but I imagined there was a lot she could do for me and help me get through this wall of mistrust. Mom told us were going grocery shopping and that her boyfriend Robert was coming over for dinner tomorrow. She continued her brief announcements about what we would be doing for Christmas and how she wanted all of to be on our best behavior. We girls looked at one another with eye brows raised wondering why the special notice. There were no issues between any of us girls and things at home are without incident.

We drove down to the Safeway on Oceanside Boulevard across the railroad tracks. It is a busy little shopping center with all sorts of shops from clothes, jewelry, pet store and a variety of other businesses. I told mom I would like to have her as my therapist and she replied that it was possible I could go under her medical card but that she would call to find out. That was even a better idea in my mind and went on to tell her I would have to get a job because my employment was denied. She asked why and I told her the situation with school and how I would be taking a class or two at night over at Mira Costa College.

There were lots all over Oceanside selling Christmas trees and I asked mom if we could have a real one this year. She said if we agreed to take care of it, watering it once a week and cleaning up after the needles fell on the floor it was alright with her. I offered to pay for it so long as we could buy it this week-end. She said she would have her boyfriend come with us and we could bring it home on his vehicle. While mom and Michelle headed off to shop Colleen and I went searching for the few items she asked us to go get. I asked Colleen what she thought of her new boyfriend and if he treated her alright?

I asked only a couple but to the point to see if there was any chance he would stick around. I asked if he drank and she replied; "*No*". Well that got him two points right off the bat. She said he was a handsome Mexican guy and maybe a year or two older then her but she seemed to like him so we'll just have to wait and see how this goes. They spend a lot of time going out dancing with Clara and her boyfriend which is how they met. He is a friend of Clara's boyfriend and they decided to set them up on a blind date. I would meet him tomorrow at dinner. I was satisfied with this information and started my prayer vigil.

The ensuing days passed like a blink of an eye. The weather was cold and I dressed as though I lived at the North Pole. I hated being cold because I had to wear layers of clothes just to be comfortable. I was happy that he was a football fan as well which meant he would most likely be watching the games and we could join him. Mother made her infamous empanadas with fedo, refried beans and ice cream for dessert. It was nearly five when I heard an engine turn off, sputtering along the path and a car door close. I opened the door to find a strikingly handsome man with dark features, hair and dark eyes standing smiling opposite the screen door.

I greeted him with a warm hello my name is Miracle, you must be Robert. His hand was warm and I searched behind him to see if there was anyone following him. I knew he had two daughters and half expected him to bring them along. Underneath the smell of refried beans and other succulent odors from the kitchen I smelt a familiar scent of Old Spice. Something dad was very fond of and wore all the time. Mom came out long enough to give him a kiss and a hug as he returned the affection. It looked awful promising to me as we followed them into the kitchen to have a seat at the dinner table.

He explained that the girls where with their mother this week-end doing Christmas shopping but that I would meet them very soon. Colleen and Michelle had already been introduced and found out they knew one another from school. We sat and said prayers before any food was dispersed upon our plates. Such a nice touch I felt and I remember the tradition from childhood. It seems this guy is old fashioned and appreciates traditional values. I miss such disciplined behavior and the sense of a complete family. They made idle talk about how work went while the girls shared the things going on in school.

I had nothing of substances to offer so kept smiling and listening to the chatter of others. Dinner was fulfilling to each of us as I told mom we would clean the kitchen and that we hoped they have a fun time tonight. She said she would probably spend the evening with him at his apartment and would be home early in the morning to go pick out a tree. She asked Colleen to get down the ornaments so we could decorate the tree this week-end. We all smiled as I ran the water to wash and Michelle cleaned the table while Colleen put away any leftovers. There was plenty of food for Matthew if he came home hungry.

We stayed up late watching television shows after we got the boxes of ornaments down from the rafters in the garage. We set the bulbs out according to color and tensile and garland off to the side. We plugged in the lights to make sure they all worked and happy to see each one of them lit right up. Everything was set and all we needed now was the tree. We all fell asleep on the couch until we heard the door open and it was Matthew. He had just come home from David's place where there was a party and he smelled of beer and pot. I told the girls to go to bed while I headed for moms room. I told Matthew to help himself to the leftovers in the refrigerator.

I mentioned to him to be careful on his way out because the Christmas lights were beside the couch along the floor. We were getting a real tree this year, picking it out tomorrow morning if he was interested to help decorate. I told him mom was staying over her boyfriend's house just in case the garage was to cold and he wanted to sleep on the couch. I was sleeping in her room. I decided to buy him very nice wool lined coat for Christmas because he was such a night owl and didn't have a decent heavy jacket for cold nights. I felt deeply for Matthew because he was having his own personal issues. He hasn't been the same since Kris died and it affected him far deeper then any of us realized.

I listened to him rustle around in the kitchen a bit longer as I thought about how I could relate to his silent suffering. I would love to have been able to talk to him but where would I start? He's always been such a private guy and not one to share his personal goings on. I know he was miserable living with dad and felt like an outcast somewhat. Mom didn't really have any choice because he was uncontrollable and she wasn't much better herself. So consequently he had no other options but to stay with dad. I resented mom for not doing something more to help him, to help herself so she could handle the situation better.

I heard the door latch close and the porch light turn off and knew that he was staying in the house. I felt better and was happy he had the sense to remain in a warm place. I thought about what I would get the girls for Christmas and would ask them for a list in the morning. I wouldn't be able to get them a lot because my funds were limited but I would ask them to prioritize their wishes. I would buy mom some nice outfits for her dates with Robert and hopes she appreciates the gesture. I wanted nothing because it's the way I am. Unless it was an article of clothing like a pair of Levis or tennis shoes I really didn't need anything.

I was never one to want. It was easier to work for the things others needed or simply helping out with groceries or paying a utility bill. Unless they could get me a car don't bother asking. Come morning we had gotten up soon as the phone rang and mom said they were on their way and to meet them outside when the horn blared. Matthew was still tucked into the couch and I told him to go sleep in the girl's room because we were going to get the tree and I need to rearrange the couch. He complied as Colleen and I moved the furniture. The horn tooted as loud as an old Volkswagen could and we raced outside to get in.

We told them good morning and that we sent Matthew to the girls room to finish sleeping. I told mom it was cold out last night and I thought it was better he stayed inside on the couch while I went to her bed. We drove along Mission down near the valley until we spotted a tree lot we liked. We looked for the fullest tree we could find that had a strong aroma of Christmas. The lots were still pretty empty at this early time of the morning which provided us with the best choices. It was a matter of fifteen or twenty minutes that we found and agreed upon the same tree and had the attendant carry it to the car where Robert secured it.

We could not be more excited then we expressed. Robert would help us take it in and get it set up in the tree stand but then he had to go pick up his daughters and would give mom a call later that afternoon or evening. We all thanked him and once the tree was standing straight we poured in the water and laid an old white sheet around the bottom for protection. Christmas was a week away and I could hardly wait. The girl's slipped me their list and I would share it with mom later to see what she suggested I get for them. I told her I was getting Matthew very nice wool lined coat for Christmas since he was such a night owl and didn't own any type of heavy jacket.

It took us until noon to finish the tree since we broke for breakfast after we let the tree stand in water about an hour or so. Mom put on the lights and she allowed us to do the rest. I would be allowed to use the car for shopping for the girls and she would do hers after work one day this week. They have this week at school before their on vacation for the holidays and will return after the New Year. We have no plans to do anything special or go anywhere for New Years Eve so I'll be hanging out here with the girls. I suppose we'll lie around and watch all the old movie marathons they show every year at this time.

Mom would be spending it with Robert, Clara and her boyfriend at a nice club with other friends. Sunday I would spend at the mall doing my Santa Claus routine and then spend the week wrapping them while the girls are at school and mom at work. It felt good to be home and I was quite excited about purchasing these gifts. I ran into a few friends from school who didn't know I was in town. I told them I had moved back and was going to Mira Costa to become a counselor. When the week resumed and the girls returned to school, mom and Matthew back to work I littered the presents over the girls bed and began the chore of wrapping.

Christmas and birthday gift wrapping is one of the happiest things I truly enjoy doing. The house drowned in the thick smell of pine tree and I loved it, we all loved it. There was a phone call that I didn't want to stop to answer but the caller was persistent. It was a woman from some company requesting me to stop in and fill out an application for employment. I scribbled down the address and asked her directions. I knew just where it was down the hill and around the corner from the Oceanside Humane Society. The name of their company was **ACDC** and it was an electronics company that made some sort of power supplies.

Things were looking up and I couldn't wait to see this place and tell mom I had an interview to go on. I had finished wrapping all the gifts and placed them under the tree by the time the girls and mo came home. They looked excited and told them they were not allowed to touch, pick up or anything else but instead would just have to wait till Christmas morning. Mom was just as excited as was Matthew when he looked underneath the tree. I hid some inside the tree and behind so they couldn't see all of them. I told mom I needed to borrow her car for an interview I had this week, she said that would be fine and could get a ride with Aunt Stella.

The girls were anxious to get out of school for the next week as I was excited about the interview. I gathered my birth certificate and any other pertinent information she requested and headed down the hill for my 7:45 appointment. I wasn't a bit nervous since I had done this before and had no doubt I could do the job. I told mom I would drop the car off to her and walk home from there so she could do her shopping. I would be speaking to a couple different people before filling out the actual application so it would be about three or so hours we would be there.

I found the location and parked on the street instead of the visitors parking. I sat for a moment before gathering my things to go inside. It is considerably smaller then ITT in Glendale but it's a job and I am grateful. We are instructed to sit in the cafeteria for a few minutes and look over the material in out packets she's handed us. Someone would be with us shortly. I didn't recognize any of the other seven or eight people sitting around the tables so I kept focused on my paperwork. There are people of all ages, shapes and sizes in this room and I felt perfectly comfortable.

An older gentleman came into the room and said he was from Human Resources and was going to get us started with the application. He gave us precise instructions and said he would return in just about twenty to thirty minutes and to have our paperwork ready by then. I was well disciplined and went right to work while I could hear others asking questions in their low voices. My work history would be simple since I only had one job. I had all the necessary information with me such as my driver's licenses and birth certificate. For those of us who had completed all the paperwork we were processed first and taken to an office to meet the next person.

Another gentleman arrived and explained he was a floor supervisor who was going to tell us what they built here. He looked over the four applications in front of him and looked up at us over his spectacles. He asked who Miracle Kelly was and I promptly raised my hand. He asked each of us what our experience was and one by one gave a little history of previous employment. He made mention of how much younger I looked them my birth certificate stated. I had the same question with my last employer. When all was said and done we were to come back the first Tuesday after New Years day and start work.

Its not likely people will start a new job during the holidays but it's all the same to me and I was thankful. We would get the particulars of wages and medical paperwork our first day during orientation and to be there at eight o'clock. Life seemed to be heading in a new direction all of a sudden. I would continue my studies at home in childhood autism and attend school this coming semester. I dropped off the car to mom and told her I would make dinner. She would be home late and just leave her a plate. I told the girls the news and they were excited for me. They would get out of school half day Friday and I told Michelle I would meet her after school.

The year ended on a positive note for me as so many things seemed to be going in the right direction finally. I would get back to softball the middle of January which meant I needed to get in better shape. I had lost another fifteen pounds and almost weight what I did when I left high school. I helped mom wrap the girl's gifts and they helped her wrap Matthews and mine. I let them wrap mothers as well. I didn't know what to get Robert and the girls so I gave mom some money and let her figure it out. The living room walls were covered with Christmas cards as was mom's tradition and looked so wonderful.

We made out Christmas Eve phone calls to family and relatives tying up the line for hours but it was all fun. We promised to come up if we could and they would do the same if they were able. The girls went to bed early as I stayed up with Matthew for a while longer. Mom went out with Robert for a while but would be home before midnight. I would be sleeping with her while Matthew stayed on the couch. I could hardly wait! Come morning the girls were first up and you could hear them rustling through their stockings. Mom got up to make a pot of coffee and told Matthew he was in charge of distributing gifts.

We would have turkey and tamales for an early dinner and snacks or cereal for breakfast. When the coffee was ready and phone stopped ringing long enough for us to gather around the tree, pleasantries were exchanged and gift giving has begun. I was overjoyed to watch the expressions of excitement and shock on the girl's faces at what they received. Matthew was ecstatic at his new coat and thanked me profusely. He wouldn't take it off the rest of the morning. Mom was surprised at her outfits as well and I was happy with my underclothes, pajamas, slippers and Levis.

The remainder of the day and rest of the week were filled with visiting relatives and friends. We went to the movies one day and basically stayed around the house the rest of the week and enjoyed our gifts. The time off was much needed and I appreciated the company of my siblings and mom. We ate turkey all week long and any other remaining leftovers. Come New Years Eve mom dressed up to the nine for her date with Robert and we wished them well. We stayed us as long as we could to watch the ball drop in Time Square with Bob Eubanks but the girls had fallen fast asleep on the floor and couch as the ten seconds started counting down.

Matthew was spending the New Year with his friend David and others so I found comfort being at home with my sisters who looked so peaceful. At the drop of the ball and the arrival of a New Year I leaned down to kiss them goodnight and woke them up to go to bed. They were slightly grumpy but only as they wobbled to their bedroom. This could be a start for a whole new beginning for me and I am anxious to see what comes next.

PERFECT IMPOSTOR

I spend the first day of the New Year 1977 entangled in the warm blankets of my bed absorbing the quite. This is my favorite time of day before the sun comes up over the East. It won't be long before the birds start their morning choir rehearsals. I find solemn peace in the innocence of the day before people awake and start the business of living. I am looking forward to working and meeting new challenges with the job. School will be just as rewarding since there is a goal associated with my reason for going. I don't want to waste my life in a factory and end up like much of the population who is stuck in these jobs for no other reason but that it's easy money.

There has got to be a higher purpose for me here then to find this type of work comfortable. I have ambitions and dreams to conduct my life in a well respected position amongst my peers whether it is teaching or youth counseling. I must seek the career of being with children in any capacity I know how. The most sought after is my passion to work with children who have been abused, neglected or orphaned. I relate better with the little people of the world and although I do not have any children of my own I will make do by surrounding myself with those who are alone.

Pursuing a higher education is very important to me and I accomplish nothing else in my life I will at least gain the respect of my family. I have learned from the best teachers in life that it's not all about what you help them to learn but the guidance and support you can give them without expectation. Mrs. Kaahaaina, Mrs. Siffing, Mrs. Collins, Mr. Nickerson and a handful of others hang in the hallway of my heart amongst the heroes of my life. They join a very prestigious group of people whom are passed on that fulfilled my life with so much love. I am by no means and ordinary girl.

I watch how my sisters interact with one another and their friends. How they conduct their relationships with their boyfriends. It is not natural for me to be with a guy in those intimate ways. It is actually against my nature to get involved any further then *just friend*. I have a history of being complicated and somewhat disconnected from other members of my family but it's how I protect my sanity. I like being alone because I'm safe. I see how my siblings have grown in my absence and how Matt has gone astray from life. I know he suffers a silent pain and seeks the comfort of drugs to ease his troubles.

I could still opt out to join the military and get my education that way for free but there are to many unknowns involved and belong exclusively to the government is not what I strive for. I can only belong to one entity at a time. My Father is enough for me and it's my choice to remain celibate and loyal to Him. I watch how the family lives together and gets along pretty good without me. It only gives me strength to save enough money and get my own place. I will see how things go once I start working and get back into softball. I am looking forward to getting back into the game again.

I'm praying hard and counting on God that He will let Robert be the one to capture mom's heart enough to marry her. Mom say's I can use the car a while to get back and forth to work until I can make other arrangements. She will either walk or go in with Aunt Stella and I can pick her up or she'll walk or ride back home with her. She only works about two miles from the house. I would see what I could come up with so I'm not dependent on her for a ride. As the girls go back to school and everybody else returns to work I get to my job thirty minutes early.

There wasn't much traffic down Mission towards the valley and since I was the first turn at the light and it was only seven thirty I had already beat the school busses and parents driving their spouses or themselves to work. Work is actually within walking distance from the house but I would have to cheek how long it takes me to drive compared to walking. I could also take the bus but would prefer walking instead. I'm young enough and have spent my life walking all over this city. I will just have to see how things go for starters. I will be nineteen on this next birthday in a couple weeks and can't think of anything I want.

I will look to see what kind of medical coverage I have to find out of therapy is covered. I am the first one inside the lobby before the other candidates and the receptionists asked my name. She mentioned it was nice that I came early while most people get her on the dot. I explained briefly that it's just the way I am to be some place before the appointed time, I hated being late and worse for others to be late. I don't wait well I told her with a smile. She quipped it was a good sign! I dressed in my most comfortable clothing of Levis and a collared three button shirt with tennis shoes.

I hadn't a clue what the job entailed but by the time eight o'clock rolled around the other five people showed up and we were escorted to the cafeteria to wait for our prospective Supervisors. Mine was named Mr. Tom Sheppard and his department was Mechanical Assembly. As he named another person we both stood up and followed him towards the receptionist where it led out a double door to the work area. I was only a little bit nervous just like I use to get in school as a child the first day. You don't know anybody and feel everybody's stares as you pass by.

He introduces me to the lead man of the department named Alfred, a slightly older Mexican guy with a bushy mustache and nice smile. He extended his hand to greet me and asked me to follow him a few steps away where I would begin my work. He introduces me to the rest of the crew on my line. One woman I take notice of particularly because when our eyes met there seemed to be a quaint greeting of an unspoken welcome. She introduced herself as Joni and I would be sitting next to her. She was very friendly as Alfred brought me a tote pan of materials and some prints to build my first job.

He explained the process of the job, how to use the material list and match it against the schematic. I was already familiar with this a little because it was somewhat similar to work I did previously. It was common sense for me to read not just the schematic but electrical drawing as well to see how the item I was building was going to work electrically. I have always done exceptionally well with my hands building things with a variety of materials. I liked making things whether it was drawing art, clay or wood construction of a small scale. Writing has been my secret passion throughout my life but building is also important.

We would have a ten minute coffee break every four hours and a half hour lunch at eleven thirty or twelve. The choice is left up to us but we would not have to clock out on the time clock which we punched in and out of before and after each shift. I looked around at others who worked in my immediate area as well as the departments across from me in the coiling department. Those folks made parts which were used to install in the power supplies my department was building. I was making nearly fifty cents more then my previous job in Glendale so I was happy about that.

I don't have any financial responsibilities yet so my money will be shared to help mom and the girls when necessary. I would open an account at one of the local banks and establish a savings for my car I will purchase when I get my income tax this year. I come to find out at the end of the day that Carl also works there and I didn't even see him until nearly the end of my first day. I was thankful to have at least one person I knew. Everybody seems to be very friendly and willing to help me with anything I might need on the job. I think I'm going to become very close with Joni Bailey who appears to be of the same nature as me.

She looks right out of the sixties with her shag haircut, shaded orange glasses and East Coast accent. I like her giggle and she smiles a lot. I am happy to report my first day was a complete success. I told Carl I would give him a call some time this week and maybe we could go out for a bite to eat, a movie or both for my birthday. I am going to be nineteen this year and have many thoughts in my head about a lot of things. I will see my therapist this week and try and come up with some sort of plan on what direction I want to take in order to set myself free from this torment I live within.

I have an urge to just sit Carl down and spill my guts but I know how he feels about me and I don't want to offend him. Even though he realizes I am not like any other girl he has ever dated before, I have a feeling he may have his suspicions. He is like my brother and he is a boy so that alone prevents any hope of intimacy between us. However I cannot forget the year in high school when I played cat and mouse with him, toying with his feelings about going out with him only to deflate his ego by denying him to get remotely close enough to kiss me. I believe it's a self protection mechanism for both parties involved.

I don't know how to begin explaining to people that as a female, I find the opposite sex repulsive to the touch. To have any sexual involvement was extremely disturbing to me because it was not natural. My relationship with Mark when I was in seventh grade and then again in high school was an exception because of an inner secret between us and by high school I was desperate to have a child and I knew that if I could get Mark to be the recipient of that child it would have a wonderful heritage and loving parents. Anything was possible back then I made enormous self sacrifices to engage in sexual exploits to create this child.

Unfortunately it was not successful and in the interim I was deeply hurt on so many levels. I saw so many possibilities for me to live a meaningful life not just as a mother but as a humane being. It has never been a question of whether I was confused about my identity or going through some teenage sexual phase. It's not even a question of perhaps being a male trapped inside a female's body. I have always been cognizant of who I am, of what I am and most especially the nature in which I exists. I have been living as an impostor my entire life and now the torment is becoming unbearable.

I cannot stop or prevent the natural state of maturing and coming of age. In the ensuing days leading up to my birthday and consequent date with Carl we had discussed certain things not so much about me personally but what had changed in my absence. I was thankful he had found a steady girlfriend which left me off the hook for trying to find ways to keep him entertained away from the thought that we could ever become lovers. He will always be my brother and nothing more. It was a rare situation when I had ever experienced a one time connection with a male due to having to much alcohol or having lost my mind as with Carl.

There had been only one occasion in which I was overcome with unexplained hormonal attraction to him in the manner of sex which at the end of the exercise as I like to refer to it, he had to pull out as not to suffer the possibility of impregnating me. I can't remember who was most disappointed, him or I. There have been more attractions for other women in my short period of time here then ever with guys in my whole life. The liaisons with men were a poor excuse for not having the opportunity to meet women of my nature and exploring my sexual appetite for them. I am not a forward type of person or inquiring about personal issues concerning their sexual preference.

I didn't know how to approach these women because I am very shy. I will flirt with another woman if she does so with me but unable to initiate the first gesture. There are women I have played ball with in my life that I've had my suspicions of but I could not bring myself to question them in private about it. There is always the risk that they aren't and would be not only highly offended but possibly repulsed at the thought of it. At therapy I am given a series of pictorial views in which I am to describe what I see in the figure. I've seen these kinds of situations on television during the soap opera days when I'd come home from elementary school to sit and watch with mom.

I never understood the significance of asking what a patient thought of a drawing that had absolutely no right answer. How does one spend endless years and tons of money to go to college and university to administer tests to determine the state of a person's mind? I don't understand how that can tell you anything about a person. I am a very simple case in my opinion. Give me the basics; give me instructions for a specific task or a list of questions and let me give the answers as best as I am able. I don't like the concept of being analyzed I guess. There are times I need to be strongly influenced into speaking what's on my mind.

My exercise was to give her an idea in our next meeting what my hopes and at least one goal I want to accomplish through this process. Ultimately I want to share in all honesty the truth about myself instead of just beating around the bush. I come in here and never know what to expect or what's expected of me. When I walk through her door and close it behind me it's like I'm two different people and have no idea which one of us is going to talk today. I'm not like that Cybil character in the same titles movie with Johanna Woodward. I don't believe I have a split personality although I have read that it occurs in severely traumatized victims, children of molestation.

I will not have myself categorized in that way because it simply is not true. I am not suffering from some kind of identity crisis like is also a favorite subject of those in the mental and psychiatric fields explaining that homosexuality is some kind of illness or reversible condition. Those in the religious sector stand beside these ridiculous claims as well and therefore are the sole reasons I no longer attend any religious organizations. Church is not a safe place for people of indifference or people like me. We are persecuted, wrongly judged and exiled from any form of religious practice because of the nature of our being.

I can never subscribe to support any church that professes to; in the name of God deny the basic principles of prayer and worship to any humane being. The God I know, the God my grandmother taught me about is a loving God and every word she spoke regarding His works have filled my heart and soul with faith. No matter what and how I suffered at the hands of those men who sexually abused me throughout my childhood and the anger which consumed me thereafter, there was a part of me that held on for the day when I would be able to question Him of His whereabouts when they what they did to me.

I struggled with each meeting in her presence because I could not share with her the pain that overwhelmed my soul. I didn't know if I was strong enough not to cry. I didn't know if I could trust her no matter how comfortable I felt. I didn't know if it was safe. I had been severely depressed when my relationship with Mark ended and I know how far within myself I journeyed. My eating habits are based on my emotional state of being. When I'm unhappy and depressed I cannot stand the sight of food. When I'm angry about something or with a family member it affects me the same way.

It's the most singular significant female thing about my character. I do not know if I will be able to force myself to keep hidden these desires to be with another woman. As January turns into to February and I have gone to H and R Block to file my income taxes it is with great pleasure that now I can go search for a vehicle of my own and cut one more string from mom for my freedom. Not that she has ever been a driving force in my life but because of our strong traditional Catholic upbringing and respecting our parents and so on and so forth it was not remotely possible for me to even consider the thought of running off like Kammillie did.

As the oldest girl it was my obligation to stand by my siblings and help as I was able. I grew up with the responsibility taught by not just family but years of family tradition as is carried on in others families of relatives. I never saw or new of any of my cousins running away from their families. I was determined to be there for my sisters because I knew the truth about mom and how she was unable to be there for them herself. Grandma taught me to be a nurturing soul, a caretaker which I have always been very proud of. My rewards would be given when I got to Heaven and it was Gods teachings that our actions spoke loudest when it came to our faith.

That was always a troublesome subject for me in the wake of my childhood sufferings. I was on more then one occasion in the palm of God's hand when in the company of a stranger and I pleaded silently with God to please take me but not let my family suffer at never recovering my body. I remember still the horrific experience of a neighborhood kid, Kristopher's best friend Danny Wright whose decomposed body was found in an empty field and we were petrified that Kristopher was left is the same condition since they both ran away together. There are some things in life that never find closure no matter how life continues.

How do I find the words to explain that I died at the age of three when my cousin Bill sodomized me? I could not bring myself to speak those words because of the enormous shame and guilt which still consumed every thread of my soul. That little girl of three still resides in the dungeon of my soul, imprisoned for the rest of my life. How do I express that? I am here ultimately to find a way to unleash this tortured child and find some way to be who I truly am without having to continue to be the impostor I portray. I disguise this part of myself very easily and without suspicion to others yet when I am alone or by myself it becomes very dangerous for me.

As my life moves on at work and socially getting back into softball with Mrs. Moore and the girls I have found my escape for now, temporary as it may be. I am fighting this mental breakdown as hard as I can because I will not allow myself to be committed to some mental institution that has power over me. I would take my life without giving it a second thought. As long as I stay preoccupied at work, with family as I am able and socially on the field with teammates everything is stable. Even dealing with the guys from work that has become friendly with me for their own selfish reasons, I have no problem telling them I'm not interested.

There are no hostile responses or angry exchanges of disappointment and we are able to remain acquaintances. Joni and I have become close over these past few months and I tell her that when I buy my car I would do anything I could to help her anytime she may need me. When she told me she was a gay woman and told me about her relationship with her girlfriend my life seemed changed forever. I had my suspicions but could not ask her directly. She also told me about the other two women, a couple in fact that everybody knew about but was not a big deal so gathered no substance for gossip.

A friend from work took me to a few car dealerships to look for a car as did mom and her boyfriend Robert. I didn't really have any particular make or model in mind but like a puppy at the shelter that picks you and not you picking the dog, I will know when I see the car. Life was moving along uneventful both personally at home and socially at work and on the field. When I finally received my tax checks in the mail I went to the bank and combined with the money I had saved from ITT I was able to get decent financing for a 1971 Pontiac Firebird, copper colored with white interior and an orange and white stripe from front to rear on both sides.

The car is five years old but it didn't matter it was mine and I was responsible for its upkeep. I was ecstatic to say the least and couldn't wait for my next therapy session. I was also paying my own way through this as well with my work insurance and not feeling embarrassed that anybody knew I was in therapy. By now I had met most of the people in the entire plane and some were parents of children I went to school with like Cindy Jones mother and my boss whose daughter I attended junior high school with. It was a big deal to have mo own car because now I wasn't dependent on any of my friends or mom.

I could come and go as I pleased and help out with the girls going back and forth to school or taking them grocery shopping. I had gathered many more feathers for my wings in preparation for leaving the nest permanently. If I wanted to see other people away from work like Joni and her friends I could do so on my own without having to borrow moms car and being held to a curfew with it. At softball there are plenty of opportunities to drive my teammates back and forth to games when there out of town. I know there will be tournaments coming up this summer in Phoenix that I'll be able to drive to in my own car.

I am looking forward to all the freedoms that go along with having your own car as well as the responsibility of maintaining it insurance wise, gas wise and mechanical upkeep. I am pretty capable of changing the oil and its filter, the air filter, thermostat when necessary, any hoses, gas filter and even change a tire. I was not afraid of getting grease and oil in my fingernails. For Michelle's birthday I gave her some money so she could buy whatever she wanted. It was easier to give them money for their birthdays as opposed to going out and buying something you didn't know if they would like or not. I took the easy way out.

For mom it was easy because I bought her nice suits for work but nothing to fancy but nice clothes she really didn't have. There was a trip planned to Glendale for Aunt Connie's birthday and Robert and his daughter were going with us. I had come to like his daughter who was Colleen's age and I liked that she was quiet like me. I thought about asking her if she liked to read poetry since she mentioned she liked writing stories. I have been writing poetry since junior high school but never share it with anybody. When I was suffering my state of depression I spent endless hours, days writing poetry as it was the only therapy I had.

I figure one day I will have the strength to share it with my therapist. There are store rooms filled with burdens that I need to share with her but it's a matter of finding the appropriate time and when that will be I cannot say at the moment. There is a married woman at work who has been flirting with me for some time but Joni had warned me about her husband who abuses her. She is older then me by about five or eight years so I will just see how things go. There is no harm in seeing a married woman whose marine husband is out of the country. It's a well known fact that he beats her from the gossip heard when she comes to work with fresh bruises and red eyes.

I don't know what drives a person to inflict harm upon another especially when it's a spouse. I don't understand either how a woman can stay and take that treatment either. I can remember when mom and dad use to fight after sending me outside with an apple and my Thumbelina doll thinking I'm going to run off and play when in reality I went directly to the kitchen window and watched them argue heatedly with one another. Dad never laid a hand on mom but she sure tried to strike him a few times but only ended up throwing things such as small appliances, drawers of silverware and serving utensils at him.

I cannot tell you how many garage doors he must have replaced during his few years that he lived in that house on Santa Anita street in Oceanside. At first I was stunned at what I saw and wasn't sure how to react since I was only three at the time and Colleen wasn't here yet. But it would not be the last time either and I just got use to the signs when I was being given a piece of fruit with my doll and ushered outside. I don't guess they ever suspected I would watch them from outside the kitchen window. I would eventually hear dad drive away and a little while later mom call me in for my nap.

I want to believe that if two people cannot get along with each other there should be no reason for them to remain living under the same roof. Children are no excuse to stay in a miserable situation. I was disappointed that dad didn't take any of us when he left and I only grew to resent him for our struggles and sufferings afterwards. We were the first and only family I knew in our entire neighborhood whose parent's were divorced and I was embarrassed. We bought mom a puppy collie as a combination birthday and mothers day gift. One of many breeds of dogs we had as children and she use to paint in oils.

She was excited and named him Lad. I first took him down to the harbor and let him feel the cool breeze of the ocean air and let him watch the seagulls hover high in the trade winds in front of us. He would stare out of curiosity but not bark. Everybody loved him and he was so energetic and playful Matthew was happy to be around him as well. There were times when he was not always in his right mind and mom was deeply concerned about his behavior. I was familiar with that deep dark place he could very well be at when he was like this. I didn't know what to do for him either and didn't know where to start.

Soon after I felt confident enough to take my therapist for a ride if she was so inclined as we took a short drive on the freeway south to Oceanside Boulevard which was the next exit down from Mission Avenue where we got on. I didn't want to be too big of a show off but I was proud of accomplishing the acquisition of my own car and declaring another step towards total independence. By now I was satisfied that the girls would indeed survive without my presence at home any longer and so thoughts of looking for an apartment with another girl began fluttering around in my head.

A couple of girls from my softball team had also expressed a desire to leave home and get an apartment we all could share. It was a though that needed exploring but perhaps closer to the end of summer or end of the year when I have a little more money saved up. Our trip to Glendale for Aunt Connie's birthday was filled with quiet moments with my siblings watching television while the adults talked in the kitchen. We had a big feast at Richard's and Betty's where the kids frolicked in the yard and us older folks hung out talking about what I'd been up to since I moved back home.

I got them up to date and told them how proud I was for finally buying my own car. I told them I was still taking night classes, Child Psychology for now and possibly some Child Development classes in the summer or fall. I was still uncertain what direction I would take. It troubled me on a personal note that I couldn't make up my mind. I felt disabled in a way and that frustrated me that I couldn't make mature decisions about my own life. I know that I wanted to get married and have children but not with a man only how do I tell them that? It was tormenting every time that subject came up and exhausted me mentally.

I thought about calling Tracy for a fleeting moment but didn't. I was afraid she would have her mother drop her off and then what would I do? I left it alone instead and engaged in idle conversations with the women in the family. I missed Cecilia and Betty most of all and of course the children whom have grown a year since I last seen them. I couldn't help but wonder how different my life might be had I stayed up here? Up to now there were no unexpected crisis or dilemmas at home to deal with so things were going okay. Aunt Connie seemed to like Robert by all outward appearances and when we left she said she would be down for a visit soon.

It was her first birthday after Uncle Felix passed and the house was not the same. With the fourth of July quickly upon us and Colleen's birthday next in line I asked her what she wanted. Colleen was never shy about anything she liked or disliked and was very opinionated. I liked that about her and how confident of herself she was except when it came to criticizing her little sister or me. She had been pretty good since she's been in therapy but there were moments of conflict between us. She is fiercely overprotective of mother still and I can't say as that's a bad thing but don't know how healthy it is.

Colleen inherited mother's temper as did I but I am able to contain my anger where she is quick to lash out. I love my sisters dearly but have never been able to figure out what it was I did or say to her that turned her against me. We have an unspoken dislike for one another that should be confronted before it gets out of control. I don't believe I would ever be able to hurt my sister physically as she had lashed out at me but then I am more a peace maker then a fighter, especially when it comes to my younger siblings. Kammillie on the other hand is a whole different story.

I will never be able to trust anything she says or does because has deceived me in the worst ways. She always has a motive no matter what her visits entail. I love her but cannot trust her and am always on guard when she's here in town. Her visit this summer with the kids this summer brought both joy and suspicion. I loved her three children and I knew she wasn't a very good mother to them but they adored her with all their hearts. I wasn't particularly happy with her comment about what happened to me that I had gained all that weight and because I was particularly sensitive about it I said nothing and instead glared at her.

Kammillie was always about Kammillie and life revolved around her. She always looked good, was thin and had the most stylish hair dos and nicest clothes. Ever since I can remember since we were little children she thought of herself as a princess and that mirror was her closest companion before boys came along. I don't envy her but feel sorry that she hasn't the heart to think of anyone but herself first. I felt most saddened for Ramona, little Mo as we called her because Kammillies was most cruel and neglectful towards her openly. I was thankful that the kids loved us and so enjoyed our company. I resented her selfishness.

I could hardly wait for the day when I would have my own family and the woman I love with me to raise them in a healthy and loving environment. Kammillie came down to have the kids spend the week end with us so she could attend some sort of seminar in San Diego for her job. I didn't ask where her husband Edie was and she didn't offer. We were just glad to see the kids again. I despised her for keeping them from us for so long without a visit. The summer was coming along fine; softball had become very exciting with our first trip to the tournament in Phoenix the week after Fourth of July.

I looked for the sewing machine Colleen asked about but wasn't quite sure which model when I got to the store. I never new they had gotten so advanced! Work was busy and finally I had met Joni's girlfriend whom they lived in a duplex down the street from the house we rented on Michigan Street in High School. It was a quaint place and I really liked how it felt, warm and welcoming. I felt confident that in a matter of time I will be able to tell Joni that I too am a lesbian although I didn't particularly care for the word. I don't like being categorized but it's what they do.

I suppose it's better then saying I'm *a homosexual, a queer* or even worse *a dyke*! God, where do these titles come from? My friendship with a married woman at work has steamed up a bit but I have not yet been able to allow myself to be seduced by her. I'm afraid because I don't have a clue of what to do or even what's expected of me. I know she believes I'm a full blown out lesbian but I'm not, not yet. I enjoy the mystery of her company and all the attention and affection she pours over me but what to do next is beyond me. I cannot ask Joni for advice because I don't want her to know I'm still a virgin where other women are concerned.

She talks about her sexual exploits as if I's been to that enchanted garden myself only I'm to embarrassed to tell I've not! I suppose that seeing a married woman as my first experience is the safest approach since there can't possibly be any expectation on my part. I cannot afford to take care of her in the fashion she lives currently and I will not be able to give her children as she's trying to conceive with her husband who I have yet to meet. I have met her bi-sexual friend Candy who I find very attractive and is fond of me as well but they have a history together and are now friends.

She warns me about getting too wrapped up or involved to deeply with her because she is a married woman and her husband is unpredictable. This I am aware of since I have seen on many occasions the bruises upon her body. I am much too young and inexperienced in these matters and therefore will not allow myself to get too far into her. I suppose what my ideal partner would be is a woman like some of the ball players we compete against. She has got to be athletic and like animals and children. I refuse to make anymore sacrifices for others and live miserable.

I gave Colleen the money she asked for to get her machine and she was finally happy with me, Thank God. Everybody seemed to be content at home and although mom and Robert had parted ways I knew it would not be long before someone else filled his shoes. I believe she prefers younger men that she can intimidate and manipulate. That's utterly shameful but it's true. Our drive out to Phoenix didn't start out very well as I needed to get my thermostat replaced and everybody was waiting at Mrs. Moore's house for us in the interim. At first they weren't sure if it was the entire radiator, the water pump or thermostat.

Next time I will take the car to my friend Jerry who owns the gas station across from the Oceanside High School who I'm certain could have diagnosed it purely by his experience as a master mechanic. If I wasn't clear across town from him here at the Carlsbad mall I could have managed to crawl back to his station. Unfortunately with the heat outside and heat of the engine I could have blown the engine and I had only had the car since March. We had hoped to get on the road early like six or seven but we didn't all get to Mrs. Moore's until shortly after eight o'clock when I needed to get something at the mall and the car acted up.

It was nearly eleven before we got going and a couple of the coaches left ahead of us. I didn't think there would be any problem crossing the desert in the heat with this next thermostat and the guy told me to make sure I had plenty of anti freeze and distilled water in the trunk just in case it started to heat up again. I was looking forward to our trip with Valerie Moore, Darlene Daligcon and Bernadette Szabad along for the ride. Once we reached Alpine, Valerie wanted to drive but I told her I wasn't comfortable with her driving since the car wasn't a hundred percent but I promised her on the drive home so long as there wasn't any problems she could drive.

For the entire week end while we were in Phoenix there was plenty of excitement and competition to be had. The heat was unbearable but it didn't stop any of us from swimming in the pool or baking our skin underneath layers of baby or suntan oil. I was no different and welcomed the little color on my untanned body. I watched intently the other players on each of the visiting teams to see if I could tell who was gay and who was not. For the most part those who were was quite obvious as they frolicked around on the grass afterwards and stayed touching one another the whole while they were at the field on the bench on in the bleachers watching.

I felt so envious of them all and ashamed that I was not being true to myself. What was I so afraid of, who was I so afraid of? I wondered where they would go at the end of the night when they were all dressed up and driving out of the parking lot. I wanted to be with them, to go where they were going because I just new there was a whole world that existed exclusively for us that only we knew where to find it. I yearned to be with others like me and did I not like myself for being the impostor I was portraying to so many others. We had not played at the top of our game for the most part and although we made it through the first round we lost the second.

It was a wonderful week-end to be away from home but now it was time to pack our things and stop by to watch the winner's bracket before we decided to head home ourselves. We had to go with the entire team because even though we were over eighteen Mrs. Moore was still responsible of us. It was the first time in a long while that we had crapped out of a round robin, double elimination tournament. We had come so far and done so poorly, I don't blame the coaches for feeling the way they did and they told us. If we continued to play at this level she wasn't going to waste her time any longer.

She was right thought and we have been playing together over ten years or longer some of us and we should be playing triple A ball but we didn't. She has every right to walk away because our effort just doesn't seem to be there like before. By the time we had packed up the cars for our venture home I told Valerie that when we made our gas stop in Alpine she could drive home from there and she was alright with that. I just didn't think it was a good idea for the disposition her mother was in to see her driving off in my car. The topic of conversation was how we did not give our best performance that maybe perhaps we should think about moving on and letting other players come in.

It would be our last season coming up anyway due to the age restrictions. We were all developing our own expectations of life and perhaps this was as far as we could go together. I was most uncomfortable with that type of talk because there were to many personal issues going on and I needed them not just as a team but as sisters which is what we really were after all these years together. Since elementary school we have been through and seen a lot together. I was not ready to disband and start fresh somewhere else. I need Mrs. Moore in my life because she kept me grounded. She reminded me of Grandmother only with Black skin.

She was short and feisty and tolerated nothing from any of us girls least of all her daughters. She not only kept my in control but doused my fire every time it got ignited. I needed her more then she could image or ever knew and I was not ready to have her exit my life. She was the only mentor I had in my life at the moment. I had plenty of time to think on the way home as I choose to sit in the back with Bernadette while Darlene sat in front while Valerie drove. I liked driving with just the sound and rhythm of the music and no talking. I wasn't in the mood any longer for conversation and I had become sullen and closed my eyes.

I was not a heavy sleeper but by the time I had woken up we had reached the house right behind her mother and then Alice and the others pulled up afterwards. Mrs. Moore asked us all to come inside for a few moments as she had something to tell us. My heart was beating a million beats per second as I was prepared for the worst. She wanted us to think, long and hard about the remainder of the season and even if we wanted to finish it out. She was pretty disgusted by our lack of effort and non aggressive playing this week-end after traveling so far to play so poorly. It was so quiet you could hear a nat fart.

She told us to show up early for practice in the morning prepared to play the way she knows we could play or let her know this was it for us. It was not possible that any of us would allow her to forfeit the rest of the season and there was no discussing it amongst ourselves. We knew better and she deserved much more then our pitiful display that went on. It was actually pretty disrespectful that we played that way and we were determined to end the season without a single loss. All us girls were there early before her and Alice showed up and already throwing balls back and forth before they reached the field.

No words were spoken and the practice continued hard and aggressive for the next two hours. Mr. Moore drilled us with hard hit grounders and long fly balls to the outfield while Mrs. Moore directed the infield in the same manner. By the end of the practice when we had all gotten a very tiring workout she had said just one sentence; *now why couldn't you have played like that in Phoenix?* No response was necessary for we all knew our guilt and left it at that. We expressed our wishes to play out our season and she alright and to be there early in the morning before game time.

For the remainder of the month and through August we had not lost a single game but come to the conclusion that perhaps this was the end of the line for this team and it was in the best interest of all of us that we move on but to certainly stay in touch. I was still not ready for our lives to come to any conclusion and I was most disturbed that I would not be seeing Mrs. Moore on a regular Saturday morning or afternoon. As much grief as I would give her over the years with my sassy mouth and out of control temper she was the only one who kept me grounded. She had become a necessity to my life and it would affect me in a terrible way.

There are some things I was not prepared to speak about in therapy especially when it affected my mental state of mind but I fear this one could not be avoided. We went from discussing the excuse of why I had started therapy, to rest assure I was of a competent state of mind to work and deal with troubled and neglected children to discussing my childhood and the incessant need of having a Mrs.

Moore in my life. There was not much to come forth in the hour since it took me so long to get started. I always came well prepared with the best intentions of sharing but somewhere between my brain and my mouth it got lost.

She suggested I write these things down. Suggested that in fact I keep a journal and write about all things that are important to me or that I need or want to share but cannot manage to get them out. It was an assignment that would come easy for me and thus I began my journey of sharing my secrets and telling the truth but only between me and the white lined sheets of paper. It would be a lonely fall season without my teammates and coaches and the years of camaraderie. My life has existed around softball since the second grade and the biggest part of who I am is through and because of sport and the girls I played with all those years.

I cannot survive without it. There would be a barbecue at the end of the season at their house and we were all expected to be there. I refused to cry in front of everybody so I put on my rubber smile and acknowledged that I'd be there. Darlene and Bernie told me that there was another team they were playing on in Carlsbad they believed I could join if I came to their next practice. I wasn't aware that you could play on two different teams in the same season. They said as long as their not in the same city it was allowed and therefore they have been doing it the past couple years now.

There was my saving grace and I knew I was going to get through this. With September here and the girls starting back in school, Colleen in the eleventh grade and Michelle in eighth I was anxious to get back to night class myself. Even mom had returned to school taking Psychology with one of my old instructors Dr. Estes. She had run into an old friend family in the same class, Terry Avila and they had started hanging around together going out after class on Friday and Saturday nights at the Casino in Carlsbad. It's an exclusively Mexican bar for dancing; drinking and any other type of entertainment people do at those places.

I was not going to be my mother's keeper no matter what the cost. I had lost a great deal already sacrificing for her wants and needs but now I see things differently. I had become pretty close with some of the people at work and spent some Friday evenings at their house swimming in the pool and partying. It was not uncommon for me to drink excessively and still believe I could be unharmed by swimming in the pool highly intoxicated. It was a rude awakening to dive in with that state of mind and not lose my breath but instead continued swimming around like a frog until I touched the bottom and headed back up to the surface.

At times I have acted in a most unfavorable and irresponsible manner but managed to survive each incident. By the time I had recovered from retreating out of the pool into some dry clothes and a towel for my hair I was feeling pretty queasy. We were all up in the room talking and fixing one another's hair by braiding it in different styles, basic braid or French. I loved the feel of another woman's hands running through my hair whether their washing it, combing or brushing it or braiding it. It was one of the most sensual feelings I could experience. Not to be confused with how mother use to massage my head as a child when she treated my hair with Alberto VO5 to make it silky and shinier.

The touch of a woman is unlike anything I have ever felt in my life and I wanted that permanently. My relationship with the married woman had nearly come close to being consummated when I stayed over because her husband was out of town but I was reluctant in the beginning. I was afraid of not knowing what to do or how to start. It was not something I neither had experience in nor practiced with anyone. No matter how strong my desires are to give in and allow her to seduce me, I couldn't. I always came up with an excuse and she didn't want to force me so long kisses and heavy breathing was the extent of our contact for the time being.

Once again I could help but think about the impact this will have not just on myself but her as well if we ever got caught, by anybody. We had gone grocery shopping a few times and looked at baby furniture and clothes for the child they were expecting this year and when we ran into some friends or acquaintances of her's, I was always the friend from work. I really liked her friend Candy and anytime she was over visiting I spent as much time as I could to talk with her. I loved her stories about them when they were younger and before they got married. I was quite taken by her and my sweetie was not happy.

I didn't care for people who became jealous or furious with me for having other people to talk to even if they are her friends. That is a ridiculous waste of emotion and energy and I do not stand for that. I've never tolerated it from former lovers and I don't plan of making any exceptions now just because she is a woman. I don't go for that and I make it understood that I do not appreciate such behavior I don't care how much older she is then me. She is a married woman and therefore has no rights or claims on my persons. I was simply having a conversation with her friend while she was in the other room entertaining guests.

I assured her that I was not accustomed to being with more then one person at a time. I believe very strongly in monogamy and even thought she is a very married woman this is a safe relationship for me with no future and no expectations on my part. I need to be sure that my being a lesbian is true with every sense of the word. I need to know that it's not just some curious phase or that I wanted to see what all the fuss was about. Being with another woman has always been my destiny for as long as I can remember since childhood. It is what's natural to me and sadly instead, I've been living as an impostor all my life.

One cannot stop or prevent the natural metamorphosis of one's life. My having been born female with predominantly male instincts has made living complicated on a variety of levels. As a child I knew that any day soon I was going to awaken and find a penis between my legs that had finally grown from my vagina. I did not comprehend that the way I was born was how I was going to remain. Most children early on don't even think about things like that but having been introduced to the tools of our bodies back then I had other ideas and issues. My life was soon filled with the endless well of distortion and fury.

I never forgot those first thoughts that flooded my head when I was being sodomized; *would he be doing this to me if I was a boy?* That question reoccurred in my mind over and over again seems like forever. I knew instinctively that God never made mistakes yet under those circumstances I felt that perhaps I must have been His first! That opinion of myself at that age, three to be specific, stained not just my heart but all my entire character as well including all thoughts and emotions. It is perhaps the single most reason why I took to reading so many books as a child and grew very passionate about doing so.

I was able to transform myself into any character I choose in the story. I also took up writing my own stories in school as well after my teachers complemented what I turned in. They would give a random subject and I took it literal enough that I played a major role in each story line. Books have always been my companions and rarely will I let one go or share them with others. If I could manage to survive all the hardships of simply living and moving on in a more constructive existence then perhaps one day very soon I may come across someone who brings comfort and peace to my world. No child should endure such insults.

Everybody at one time or another gathers baggage along the way and I'm no different. I just manage to keep mine deeply buried inside where it cannot be uncovered. My shield and my armor are so thick that only God my Father is able to penetrate them. It takes a lot for me to cry and I don't see things like an ordinary female. I rarely relate to the raw emotions of a woman and am not easily intimidated. You can offend me, criticize me, even threaten to get physical with me, I will remain calm but the moment you lay one finger upon my person it could very well be the end of one or both of us.

When Colleen and I are in a heated conflict I have to force myself to remain calm and not allow my temper to override my better senses. We are both extremely intense individuals but she is much more impulsive then I. I am always cognizant of the consequences involved where she is outright emotional and will react rather then think. I am more aware of my strength then she knows and therefore I could never physically accost her. I may at any point defend myself, family or friends when trouble arises but if it is someone I know rather then a stranger I will do everything I can to talk my way out of a confrontation. I will attempt diplomacy first at any cost.

I know to well my potential for disabling another if I get backed against the wall. It's humane nature to defend yourself when the threat or danger of bodily harm is upon you. If the war of words can not be settled or broken I prefer to walk away rather then pursue an endless procession of verbal debating. I don't like conflict in any relationship, personal or social and I will not stand for it for to long a period of time. There is no winning in arguing with a woman. I will be the first to tell you how passive I am when it comes to disagreements. I prefer to find compromise in a relationship and be filled with love and compassion rather then mistrust and discord.

I have had a lifetime of heartache and misery already in my young life and I cannot absorb anymore. I refuse to be involved with someone, a married woman at that, who insists I belong to or am exclusive her's alone. I cannot express strongly enough that I belong to no one except God and any relationship I enter into as far as I'm concerned is because that's where I'm superposed to be at the time. My goal in life is to have one and only one partner to spend the rest of my life with. I want to meet a woman whom we can grow together in a loving relationship without losing our own identity or giving up any part of ourselves.

I don't come with expectations because then you invite imminent disappointment. I have many acquaintances and only a handful of friends. I think of my friends more as sisters and brothers' rather then friends, their more endearing to me then that. I don't feel like I belong in the family I was born into ever since that first experience because I was damaged in such a way that I felt orphaned by the silence that engulfed me afterwards and every incident that occurred thereafter. Who could I go to, who could I tell? I was a child and adults don't have time to hear the grievances of children especially when what they were saying was impossible to comprehend.

The dungeon of my soul was the only safe place to reside away from others and still pretend like I was a part of the family. Nothing was different, nothing had changed. I was jailed by fear and consequently my heart hardened and a more protective person took control of my disconnected life. I have never had successful intimate relationship for obvious reasons in that I have forced myself to be something I am not no matter what I appeared on the outside. There are many people tormented by the places they are forced to hide. I was afraid mom would have me committed to some institution to have me fixed or at least get it shocked out of me.

I watch at work how people interact with the known lesbians and it isn't any different then how they interact with anybody else. They aren't treated indifferently and I was proud to be such a close friend to Joni because in reality we were just like one another only she was out and I was well hidden in a sense. She knew, she told me that she saw it right away. It may have been obvious to her but not anybody else. I was ashamed to be hiding when there really was no reason for it. She tried as often as she could to encourage me to stand up to my mother and confront her with the truth which she guaranteed me she already knew about.

I promised her I was working on doing just that through my weekly therapy session. She asked me how long I planned on milking those excuses before I let it go? It just wasn't that easy for me because of all the complications. I didn't want to share the horror of my childhood with her because then she might think those experiences turned me into a lesbian and I didn't want to have to explain or try to justify my preference to her or anybody. It's the single most reason why I choose not to discuss my abuse with my therapist at this point because I don't want her to presume that this is more a condition as a result of the abuse and not how I was born.

I don't want to spend my life feeling like I have to justify my sexuality to everybody. They will not understand nor believe that this is how God created me and not because of years of being sexually violated. Then I would have to take a real look at myself and realize how shattered my life truly is and that I really don't like me. I have taken great steps to cover up and mask the pain and agony I suffer on a daily basis. It's as if I'm raising a disabled child within that suffers such bouts of depression and heartache that many times it takes alcohol to ease the nightmare in which I live.

Terry, as many of my relatives refer to me is one person and Miracle is yet another. We are a *two spirited* individual as some American Indian tribes consider gay people because they have both female and male spirits living in perfect harmony. There is something about the American Indian culture that has always fascinated and enchanted me. I respect how they consider the entire planet as Mother Earth and all things upon it are sacred. Unlike any other culture I'm familiar with, they treat the land with utmost respect and do whatever is necessary to preserve and purge anything spoiled from it.

It is not in their nature to destroy and deplete its resources as that of other cultures. I grew up all around Oceanside all my life and now see how things are changing rather rapidly. I hear it is for the sake of progress and one cannot stop the natural progression of such occurrences yet I will be the first to disagree. How many shopping centers, grocery stores and car dealerships can, must one city have? I am an instinctively empathetic individual who will come to the aid and defense of those who have no voice and cannot defend themselves against a greedy society and money of corporate America.

I do not throw my two cents into every debate about politics or religion because they are worldly things that my Father says we need not be worried about and don't trouble one's self over. I know that in the end of all this living we will have one person to answer to ultimately and that's God. I see that life is not about how much you have, where you live, who you are but more what you do with your life and the blessings He has bestowed upon you. I was never in a hurry to grow up like many of my school friends. I never wanted to be like someone else either. I didn't know how much longer I would be alive.

My constant fear was always the continuation of life itself not the people or things I came into contact with on a daily basis. Most people I know are afraid of death while I embrace it. It was the only certainty of lasting peace that I knew was real. When I get depressed or angry I resort to self mutilation because the pain I cause would be strictly upon myself and not others. My threshold for pain is enormous and more then not I could barely feel it anyway. I keep a razor with me at all times much like men carry condoms. I do not cut myself where it is visible to others and I don't have to worry about hiding the scars.

I could only share superficial wounds with my therapist for the time being because the longer I went to see her the more I realized I had bigger problems then I could ever admit to a stranger. I didn't know the extent of her power over me and thus kept my personal hell to myself. It was going to be a long while before I would be able to share the more horrific elements of my self to her. I didn't know what to expect out of her each visit but it was not initiated until I spoke first. If I truly needed help with something I had to give her some idea of what it was, any clue was better then silence.

October had come and gone and now Thanksgiving was soon upon us and I felt excited to be able to participate in preparing the dinner, buying the food and everything else that comes along with the holiday. In all my life's sadness I truly came somewhat alive around the holidays. There were always children to make happy and give something to. I took great pleasure in going beyond ordinary to shower them with gifts and surprises, mom included. I may not be the best daughter out of the four but I still remain the most faithful. Work was busy and I had put in some overtime hours during the month which allowed me to save a little extra.

Matthew and I helped as much as we could with household expenses and things for the girls but most of the time mom was able to keep us above the waterline. Dad continued to send the little child support he did each month until the girls turn eighteen but we still struggled none the less. It would be so much easier for all of us if mom would choose a man capable of taking care of her and willing to help out her kids as well. I know that if she ever settled down with someone decent and married him that Matthew and I would move out and leave them to their happy little lives, just them and the girls.

Perhaps that is a fantasy that may never come true but I keep hoping, keep praying. I have been so inclined throughout my life to express my true feelings amongst my closest friends but then there was the possibility of rejection, or ostracized by not just my closest allies but anyone they might tell. There is no one single person of any significance in which I can confide which increases my burdens ten fold. I know in my heart that mother really knows what kind of person I am but cannot accept, will not accept that one of her children is homosexual as she so disgustingly refers to them.

It is true without saying that no parent wants a homosexual child and they are repulsed to even think about it. I carry not just an enormous amount of guilt and shame but fear that the loss of family connections will undoubtedly leave me asocial. I've always been somewhat of a recluse in my private life and only when I'm around my teammates do I truly feel comfortable. I look forward to the start of a new season and joining new teams. I will play with the Cerda Brothers in Oceanside and the Breakers in Carlsbad. Colleen will join me on the Cerda Brothers team along with girls I attended school with.

Ralph is the coach and his wife Becky also plays on the team, she is the sister of Bill's wife. I have flirted once or twice with the notion of talking to her privately but once again fear got the better of me. Nobody ever seemed to mind or criticize me for being a tomboy yet instead appreciated my skills. On the Carlsbad team where I also played with many girls from Mrs. Moore's team there were others I felt suspicious about but could not approach. I didn't know what the stereotypical lesbian looked like and just because many women in softball are exceptional players and may look gay they aren't.

I was looking forward to the coming season where I would be busy all weekend and twice during the week depending what night my teams played. It was the sole activity that kept me going for the time being. I backed off a bit from seeing my companion for fear her husband would find out. I didn't know how to be discreet about sneaking around with his wife no matter how safe it appeared. There was just so much going on in my head that I found it difficult to breathe some days. He appeared to be growing suspicious with every visit she tells me. Thanksgiving eve had arrived and Colleen and I were organizing the menu and who would help with what mom requested of us.

There was a choice of peeling, mixing, cleaning or preparing certain dishes. Mom of course would prepare the stuffing which was not from a box and cook the turkey. Matthew and David were out in the front yard talking with friends and having beers. I would share a small glass of port wine or sherry with mom as we began the process of preparing for the morning. There is celery to chop, onions to cut and potatoes to peel. Michelle and Colleen did what they liked best as I picked up any slack. I had spared nothing in getting the biggest, plumpest fresh turkey that I could order from Vons and made sure it would still be tender.

Aside from fresh flour tortillas my second most favorite smell was oven roasting turkey. I loved this time of year when our family has managed to set aside our feelings of discontent with one another and opened up our hearts to be grateful that we're all together. The holidays always take me back to my childhood when times were happier and the family complete with dad. It was a gigantic production back in those days and a time where mom just had to worry about what dishes to set out and what to wear. Because dad was the head chef on base he prepared the entire meal at work and brought it home in shifts.

Feeding a family of seven growing children could be a major task in itself but he always managed to pull it off without incident that I can recollect. I made the mashed potatoes and biscuits while the girls retreated to their room once their part was completed. It was a cold November morning and perhaps a few scattered clouds were hanging around over the ocean and mountains. *Could be rain I thought and what a comfort that would be.* As joyful and festive a day as it is, the sense of melancholy still creeps into the back of my thought. At a time when we are praying in thanksgiving for all the blessings we have, I contemplate exposing my truth.

I hold off because of the special day that it is and for once we're altogether and getting along. We get phone calls from relatives wishing us Happy Thanksgiving and that maybe they will come down for the week-end and visit weather permitting. I can only imagine how lonely it must be for Aunt Connie to spend her first holiday without Uncle Felix but she is surrounded by her three children and their children. A full house I can imagine with nine children running around. We sit around watching the football game while dinner is cooking and mom informs us we should be eating around two which turned into an all day experience.

It was the first time in a long while since my return that I've felt content amongst my siblings and mom. There is still some hesitation and reservation about my responsibilities here and when I should think about moving on but for now I stay put. Christmas is a huge holiday for us and I'm looking forward to getting the girls, Matt and mom what they want or at least one of the things they want. In my life it's all about giving and not saving for a rainy day. In my opinion and at the rate my life has gone, there may never come a rainy day that I'll need all that money I've tucked away.

Life is temporary and one never knows for certain if they will awaken from the nights sleep. Once dinner is ready we call the girls in from outside and take our places at the table. Mom has her boyfriend Andreas, a very young Mexican national, sit beside her while Matthew and David sit at the opposite end of the table and the girls and I fill in the empty chairs. He is nearly half her age but they seem to get along alright. She met him one Saturday when she and Terry were out dancing at the Casino in Carlsbad. They drink a little too much for me but then who am I to tell them anything, after all, their adults.

Matthew cuts the turkey since he's the man of the house and Andreas is more like a guest until mom gets tired of him too. For the next couple of hours or so we talked about a lot of things from what and how the girls were doing in school to what Matthew had been drawing these days. As he's grown up his art work has gone through many changes and genres. He prefers American Indian paintings and animals to landscapes as mom used to draw. They both are very talented artists and I wish they had pursed a career in that. We all seem to have our hidden talents, them with their drawing, Colleen who is very talented with woodworking and me with my writing.

Michelle I believe is still in the searching stages of her creative talent not pinpointing any one thing in particular. I will go back to school to finish off the semester in Child Psychology where we're studying Autism. I won't go for my AA degree because I'm still uncertain what direction I will go. I prefer to continue with my home studying and try to narrow it down whether I want to teach or counsel. I just know I want to be involved with cultivation and enriching the lives of children. At the end of our meal we girls clean up the kitchen while the guys decide to go back to David's and mom and Andreas go dancing.

It has become quite difficult of late to continue making excuses about my friend and why I spend so much time with her. Aside from being both married and preparing for their adopted child I explain that we're just really good friends. I have a friend from work who is a Black man and very sweet that has a thing for me which bothers mom I can tell. I assure her that we are work buddies and tell her he's married with a small child. It disturbs her that as I mature my companions are women and not men. I would think it would be clearly obvious to her exactly where I stand. Neither of my sisters ever questions me about them or Matthew either for that matter.

When I get upset I'll take the dog for a ride down to the beach by the pier and just sit. I love how the ocean calms me and how the rhythm of the waves is similar to how I inhale and exhale. Sometimes I really need to be absolutely by myself and not talk to anyone. I am beside myself when mom and I have a falling out and it happens so often. I find it disturbing that I cannot share these episodes with my therapist. I'm sure she could help me find out or understand where the anger comes from which would in turn lead me to sharing my past. All things in a person's life are rooted in the beginning like it or not. Very few realize the impact childhood has on your adult life.

When I'm not playing ball twice a week or at school on Monday nights I remain alone with whoever in the family is home. The girls usually have homework and Matthew is at David's. I spend time with the dog who is growing quite fast since we got him in May. He will be a year old in January when I turn twenty. *God is that scary!* I do a little babysitting for Richard and Betty when they ask or I'll let Michelle take the job. She could use a little extra money for things she wants for school. I've decided to buy mom some additional work suits for Christmas and the girl's bedroom furniture, bunk beds.

I will purchase art supplies for Matthew who can never have enough. After Thanksgiving we moved into buying Christmas cards and thinking about whether we wanted to get a fresh Christmas tree or not. It was the most hectic time of year and I really needed the distractions. I kept myself busy so I wouldn't have time to look back on how disappointed I was about my current status. It's my number one goal to come out this year no matter what the consequences. I can't continue pretending to be like an ordinary girl. I can't relate and I have needs and desires of my own.

My teammates are the foremost type of women I spend my time with on week-ends unless mom needs me for anything or the girls need me. There are plenty of gay women softball players around the league who are gay but nobody makes a big deal about it. I talk to Joni a lot about what I should do and questioned her about her personal life, when she knew, how old was she when she told her parents, how did they react? I guess I just needed someone to tell me it was alright and that *NO, God was not going to strike me dead!* I know I must be a huge disappointment to Him for not turning my life around but I don't know how I would have done that.

This is not a disorder of some kind or some psychological condition that can be cured with medication or shock treatment. It is how I came into this world. It is my nature and if I am going to survive this miserable life I need to be honest not just with myself but my therapist and family as well. I realize I have deeper issues within myself that need immediate attention as well but getting the words out of my mouth has its own dilemmas. I am constantly in crisis with myself and have no clear means of reconciling. I have spent my life protecting that little girl who resides in the dungeon of my soul to the point that I neglect myself.

We go through the ritual of finding an acceptable Christmas tree and decorating it. I will have to set my problems aside for now and get on with the business of giving. The girls are out of school for the rest of the month and I have taken care of paying and making arrangements to have the girls bunk beds picked up. Mom's clothes and Matthews's art supplies will be wrapped by the girls while I manage to figure out how I'm going to tell them about their beds. I don't ask for anything and just leave mom to her own devices when it comes to buying for me. I have my books, softball equipment, bats, gloves, cleats and a car so I'm pretty settled.

Perhaps a nice cross or religious medal would suffice as I can't think of anything I might need. I know money is tighter this time of year and this holiday especially is for children even if they are now teenagers. I have a job so helping mom out with gifts isn't a problem and Matthew always gives mom money because he hasn't a clue what to get them. Besides, shopping is such a girly thing to do. If he needed anything in particular he would let us know. Mom usually got him a couple pairs of Levis and socks which he was very content about. He still wore his wool lined coat I got him last year and not yet ready for another.

I loved waking up to the smell of pine in the house and the swift cold air that enveloped us all before someone could put the wall heater on. I couldn't tell who was most excited, the dog or the girls. They first rifled through their stockings which had shrunk considerably in size none the less now filled with school supplies like writing utensils, erasers, a toy or two and incidentals such as toothbrush, dental floss and the likes. I was still overcome with emotion just watching their expressions as they ripped apart the wrapping and smiled with each gift. I sat in awe as happiness and surprise blanketed their faces.

Even Matthew managed to flash his pearly withes underneath that wavy long hair of his. I had the distinct pleasure of unwrapping a nice new glove and other softball necessities which surprised me because I am very particular about my bats and other equipment I buy. Mom said she kept the receipt just in case I wanted to exchange anything. I thanked her for everything and said *it was just right*. We started to get cleaned up a bit while the girls put their presents away and the remainder of the gifts which were for Andreas would be opened later when he came over.

I gave the dog his new toys and would take him for a walk just after breakfast. The phone rang off the hook shortly after we cleaned up the living room and it was our cousins who said they would be by later this morning to visit. Everyone had made plans for how they were going to spend New Years Eve and I was happy the girls decided to stay home instead of spend the night with their own friends. I liked being at home because it was safer. There was usually a bottle or two of wine in the cabinet if I wanted to celebrate with a drink and I would allow the girls to have some if they wanted as well.

Fortunately neither one of them cared for the taste or the after effects so I would be drinking alone. I had been invited to spend the evening with Joni and her girlfriend whom were going to a party but I declined preferring to stay home, perhaps maybe next year but for now I wanted to be with my sisters. Crazy things always happened this time of year so being in my own home assured I wouldn't get into any mishaps. I was getting more and more concerned about Matthew though because he had been behaving peculiar these past few months. I know David watches out for him but he's been deeply troubled.

I was looking forward to a quiet night at home as the girls cuddled together on the couch beside the Christmas tree which still smelled of pine forest. I lay on the floor with the dog as my pillow and a blanket over my body. I don't think I would ever want to live my life without the companionship of an animal. We grew up will all sorts of animals and a lot of them so we were never without a pet. Our pets have been like members of the family, more like a sibling then an animal and I have found tremendous solitude in their presence. If I had to make a choice between humane and animal, it would surely be the animal without question.

The hour has arrived and once again my sisters have fallen off to sleep by eleven forty five and I am content to celebrate the New Year with the next best thing, our dog Laddie. He has been a Godsend to me even thought he was a gift for mom. We are the perfect couple he and I. Laying here awaiting the sounds of firecrackers to erupt any minute. I say a little prayer of Thanksgiving and ask God to give me the strength to tell the truth and end this life of intolerable lies. The girls woke up almost instantaneously as soon as the firecrackers went off and people drove by honking their horns and screaming Happy New Year.

I hope indeed that this year will be a happy one as I look forward to taking the plunge and telling my family, friends and therapist the honest truth. I wrote quite a few verses in my tablet which I had started some months ago. It is different then the journal I began after my therapist suggested it. This one is strictly poetry. I will remain on the couch while I have the girls go to bed and knowing Matthew will stay the night at David's. There are no new expectations for me to think about or wish upon for the New Year except finding a way to break free of my tormented existence.

THE HONEST TRUTH

New Years day 1978 was filled with an abundance of company and a family member or two dealing with hangovers. I know times they are a changing. I made a promise not just to God but myself as well. I will start this journey and embark on a path that for all intense purposes will allow me to be open and honest with mom, my siblings and friends. My closest companions I shall reserve for later when I see what the reactions are from my immediate family and closest friends. It's as though I've backed myself against a wall and there is no place to run, hide or escape. After all, what am I afraid of?

I also find it somewhat disturbing that I have a clear vision of what I want to do with my life but not a visible path to obtain or achieve such results. I have grown up protecting this little girl and although I harbor no ill feelings towards her, she does seem to be the root cause in prohibiting me from getting on with my life. I have every intention of revealing my sexual identity to my therapist as well and perhaps first to see how she reacts. I'm not so much afraid of how people will respond rather then what their first words will be. I am an individual without expectations and therefore can't begin to image what their feelings will produce.

I am prepared for some amount of rejection which is what I expect first and foremost, even physical contact perhaps but to be denied by any of my family members would shock me. If anyone knows the kind of person I am, always have been, it is my immediate family. Doesn't matter that I have an intense personality in one respect and fiercely loyal in another, I hope they see me still as the ever loving, ever empathetic individual I have always been. First reactions tell the whole story. I need to find the right time and place in which to initiate the conversation and I would prefer to do it when everyone is present.

At work I have shared this with Joni whom is all supportive of me and has offered me a place to stay if things go badly. Deep down I truly expect things to go badly because I don't come from a loving, understanding environment at home. Mother has many deep rooted racial issues and it's off the scales when it comes to homosexuality. I have watched her facial expressions whenever a story came upon the news concerning the subject most particularly when it was broadcast in June when most of the state wide parades took place. I always made it a point to watch as much of and anything pertaining to those events.

My heart tells me she has always known but is in a deep state of denial and may never be able to accept it. I don't know why it's so important for me to have her approval or acceptance because we are the furthest from being mother and daughter that you could get. I see us as two women who reside in the same house nothing more. I know she won't be receptive to the truth no matter when I tell her so it's all about how I break this news. This is my biggest dilemma and one I cannot resolve on my own. If there was a support group I could find that would be a great source of support but how would I go about looking for them?

I have to wonder; have to ask myself; how many other people live such a tormented existence as this? What is all the fear about? Where does the anger come from? Are people so ignorant and prejudice that they cannot give their child the same love as they have since conception? How does a parent cut off their child because of who they are? I realize that anger breeds fear, fear breeds ignorance but there comes a point when a parent must accept that this is the same child who made you laugh at their childhood antics. There is nothing traditional about homosexuality if you choose to see it that way. Truth is, God loves everybody and it's our conduct He questions.

You don't stop loving someone because their not like you. What are they comparing their opinions to? Is it that they don't know their child well enough to see that they have raised a loving, nurturing humane being? Who cares that they are attracted to the same sex? What does it matter? These questions burn holes in my heart when it comes to the thought of confronting my family. I have to tell the honest truth because I can no longer continue hiding as I do. So I must ask myself, what is my fear? I will be twenty years old this month and I am shocked at still being alive. As much as I fight myself to remain in this miserable world I have to stop and look around and wonder why.

I look in the mirror and see the distant shadow of a small child that I have never been able to put to rest. She is only three years old but holds all that I am in the middle of her palm. I cannot seem to escape her hold of me. I look at my life and ask what other sacrifices do I have left to make for my family. What are the risks at coming out? I know the strong traditions of the family as well as the history. My cousin Johnny from San Diego is openly gay and he was the first high school student to take his boyfriend to the prom. His mother used to be a nun. I know they have a descent relationship to say the least.

If there is anyone who could offer the most support for both mom and I, it's Aunt Rose. There is the remote chance that mom may have discussed this with her in the past, I can't be sure but they have always been close out of the six sisters that there are. How does one approach such a sensitive and delicate matter with a parent whom you know alarmingly disapproves of such people. The more I think about it the worse I feel and it's become mentally exhausting. I know there will be a way to deal with this, there has to be. We did the family celebration things with a nice dinner at home and cake and ice cream afterwards.

I was feeling just a little better about myself because I had dropped another fifteen pounds since being home which I'm sure was partially due to stress. Softball is the only thing basically that keeps me sane. I had lost my enthusiasm in class and decided at the conclusion of the semester I would not return for additional courses. Although I am a great believer of education it had become evident to me I was not going to pursue a career in teaching. The cost of books and length of time, years it would take me by going to school at night was unacceptable to me. I wasn't going to collect unemployment to attend school to be a teacher so I choose to end it.

I still saw my married friend who by now is awaiting the arrival of their son soon. I had gone to K-Mart and picked up a few articles of baby furniture and some clothes for the occasion and delivered them to her and her husband that week-end. Her brother in law was in town and she invited me over to attend a barbecue they planned for him. I had met him briefly before and he had mentioned my name this visit so it was nice I would visit him. I was still pretty shy and kept a low profile in crowds when I didn't know any people so this party was no different. There were a select few from work but most were strangers.

He asked me if I wanted to go for a drive with him and another young couple and I said sure, I would drive. He was here on leave from the service and I found him to be quite pleasant to talk to. He wasn't the typical guy who wanted to talk about nothing but him so it was nice to be driving around the beach and ending up by Buddy Todd Park. It was still a popular hangout for teenagers and such so we pulled to a spot that looked North over the valley and we could see the drive in from there. I spent many a day here playing with friends and family growing up and I have some fond memories.

Oceanside was beginning to change in a way that I didn't care for. As a military town there were often new families moving in and out as the husbands were relocated or shipped out on deployment. I was thankful that dad spent his last years in the Marine Corps at Camp Pendleton and we didn't have to worry about uprooting our lives to accommodate his career. They did enough of that when Kristopher and Kammillie were born in Kodiak Alaska. I loved the rural landscape of this city but now this thing called expansion of almost every sort was moving in quite rapidly.

I miss the open spaces and hate seeing the building going on all around us. Perhaps this is why I am so drawn to spending so much time in the mountains when I am able. When things are tough for whatever reason I will sometimes take the dog and drive up to Palomar Mountain and breathe. I would also do the same by going to the beach and experiencing the same emotions. I cannot function properly amongst the general population because there's too much noise. I could live in a tent and be perfectly content just me and the dog. I'm finding that as I get older the need for socialization outside of softball is less.

They light up a joint and I am hesitant in the beginning. I haven't smoked pot since high school and didn't know what it would do to me now. Back then there was a purpose for getting wonderfully intoxicated but those reasons have changed and I was unsure how my mind and body would react. I have a very low tolerance for alcohol and drug consumption so after a few hits I can feel myself begin giggling at every story they tell. I got one of three ways; happy, horny or hungry and I am thankful this stuff affected me happily. We sat around storytelling although I mostly listened.

Since I was driving and spoke up that we should be going because I had to work the next day they agreed without question. I had no idea what time it was but only that I was extremely high and very nervous about driving back to the house. I knew it was late but not past midnight. The weather was cold but since I was numb it really didn't affect me that badly. I was wearing my long sweater which kept me well insulated from the elements. I kept aware of my speed and watched the odometer closely as I maneuvered the streets until we reached our final destination.

I had gone inside with the others to say my good nights and hug my friends. The party was still going on pretty strong but the music was slightly lower due to the time. I was still pretty high when I got back in the car and her brother in law asked if I was sure I was okay to drive home. He offered to drive me and his friend would follow but I assured him I only lived a few miles from Buddy Todd and I would be home in fifteen, twenty minutes. It was sweet of him to ask but I was confident I could get home without incident. I was not in the habit of driving while intoxicated but I kept the window down and drove as quickly but carefully as possible.

Since the couch was unoccupied and mom's car was in the drive I decided to sleep there. The garage light was still on so I knew Matthew was home. The week-end was spent playing ball and a little private time writing. I spent that quality time with our dog and either watched television if it was not occupied or drove some place quiet to sit. The beach was always first choice. I didn't give my promise to God any thought since I didn't know quite how to approach the situation yet. Therapy was going well but I still couldn't bring myself to telling her either. I can't begin to tell what's preventing me from saying those words, I'm gay.

At work Joni and I continued to talk about all sorts of things from relationships she's had in the past and generally what life's like being lesbian. I found our conversations very educational and she filled my head with endless hope. We have a mutual friend who had found a better job that paid more and asked us if we were interested in applying for any of the openings they had. I inquired further and felt that it would be a good opportunity to save more money to eventually move out. It was in Santa Ana but they had a shuttle that many people in North County took each day. They work a four forty week, four days ten hours a day, the biggest attraction for me.

Ultimately that was the clincher and I called the number she gave me when I got home. I talked to Michelle mostly when I was going to make any changes in my life because she was pretty good about listening to me. It is important in life for a person to have at least one ally in the family amongst their siblings. Michelle is the youngest and I have always done everything I could to protect her from Colleen and mom when she was being mistreated or neglected by either of them. She and Colleen have always had a kind of convoluted relationship every since I can remember because their personalities are so extremely different.

Michelle is rather quiet, almost meek in comparison and not so much in need for mom's attentions. Colleen on the other hand is quite the opposite in that for whatever reasons she has always been jealous of the relationship between mother and I. I couldn't explain to her in any clearer fashion that there is absolutely no existing relationship between us never has been and quite frankly never will be. There are so many things which have occurred between mom and I that separate us for a lifetime that cannot possibly be reconciled. I have deep rooted resentment for mom that cannot be explained to Colleen because of her relationship with mom.

As children she used to play Michelle against mom and I for which enraged me to no end because mom didn't see it or at least didn't want to see it. Therefore our relationship has always had some degree of contempt. It has been very difficult for me over the years once dad left and our family quietly and suddenly began to deteriorate. Even in the midst of living in a dysfunctional environment we still co-existed as a family until dad began spending more time away from the house due to the problems in their marriage. Staying together for the children was certainly not an option for them any longer.

I was anxious to live my own life if possible and I looked for assistance from therapy and friends in which to take that inevitable leap. I made the call and set up an appointment to be interviewed where I would take a sick day. I wasn't one to miss work or take vacations because I never went anywhere. I was a loyalist at work as well so I banked my accrued vacation and sick days for a rainy day. I loved the idea of working four days a week ten hours a day leaving me three days to do whatever I wanted. I would miss Joni and a select few others but I knew where to reach them if I left.

I had become fairly close with a few people and their families over the past year and we had some wonderful times barbecuing on week-ends and such. I don't know if or how it would effect my week night ball games but I'll have to see. It all depends on whether or not I qualify for the position. I informed Michelle about the proposition and she encouraged me to go for it. My girlfriend says I should do whatever I needed to improve myself and get ahead. Life at home had continued unchanged with the girls in school, mom working and playing on Friday and Saturday nights either with Andreas or Teresa.

I was happy that she continued her classes at night school and was hoping that information would effect the decisions she was to make with the girls as time went on. It was a course she took that would affect her pay on the job. She needed the educational background for her certificate and eventually a degree in Child Development. I was happy that her job at the center was going well and there where no problems between her and Aunt Stella. It can sometimes be tricky when family work together but she and Aunt Stella have managed to have success in their endeavor together.

There was a time when Aunt Stella and I suffered a disconnection of sorts after the death of Kristopher and mom decided to sale the house. For obvious reasons I took that move the hardest because I didn't want to move for numerous reasons from not wanting to leave the memories to being displaced from all my child-hood friends. I had become resentful of mom for the continued decisions she made without at least including our feelings in the matter. I was not looking for-ward to the life changes that were going to occur. Aunt Stella and I had a falling out because it was such an emotional time for me and I took it out on her.

I could never have developed any decent relationship with her even thought she was my God Mother because of the history with her son. I see her and I see William all over again and those pent up feelings of fear and torment come flood-ing back. So I never get very far away from what happened because our families see one another often. It's a reminder I cannot escape from. As much as I want to tell her, I can't. I still baby-sit for him on occasions but not as much as I use to, I'm getting to old for that and I let Michelle or Colleen take the job instead. I often wonder what goes through his head when I take care of his kids.

Does he ever think about what he did to me and feel the least bit guilty or ashamed? Does he realize the impact his actions had on my life? He has three daughters of his own and I cannot escape the thoughts or question if he's done the same thing to any of them. I will always be that three year old little girl no matter how many birthdays I continue to have. She remains the child I can't seem to have and therefore remain childless no matter how hard I tried to conceive. It's just another heart breaking disappointment in my life. The older I get the less desire I have to want a child of my own because of what and how I'd have to get impregnated.

The day of my interview came and went and fortunately I passed every test they required of me to become their employee. I would be joining their company mid February and give my boss two weeks notice when I returned to work the next day. I filled out the necessary paperwork, medical information as well as personal data and received the schedule for the shuttle which I will take back and forth for a small fee. We would be picked up at the Gemco shopping center off El Camino Real near Vista Way in Oceanside. I would leave my car there in the parking lot next to the others who share the ride.

My new company name is *EATON/LEONARD Corporation* out of Santa Ana but they are in the process of relocating to Carlsbad next to Anthony Pools on El Camino Real. They produce computerized tube bending machines which I have seen at a glance because it was at another location across from their small building. It is a fairly new company less then five years old and they are now growing at an alarming pace currently and therefore looking for experienced, qualified workers. Most of their workforce lives in and around Santa Ana but have chosen to follow them to Carlsbad on a shuttle they will provide from that end.

I have had a most wonderful if not educational thirteen months with ACDC and made some exceptional friends there. It has taken nearly three months before my girlfriend and I experienced another sexual encounter if you can call it that. She initiated the intimacy by having me just lay back and enjoy it. Her husband was away on military business and wouldn't be home for the next thirty days or so. It was something I could not share with Joni because I would never hear then end of it. She too was once hit upon by my girlfriend but Joni knew better and has more self-respect for herself then to be seduced by just any woman.

I was nervous to say the least because I had absolutely no idea and less experience at what was about to occur. I had an idea and the natural response came with any touch but she dominated the encounter and as she instructed; I remained passive and allowed her to show me what it was women do to one another in intimate situations such as this. There were no words to describe the emotions that flooded my mind and body and I was left speechless through the entire experience. I was not allowed to explore my own curiosity this time around but she did agree to my insistence upon cupping her for the rest of the night naked.

I am not one to part from my partner after such an exhausting display of affection because I do not want to lose the overwhelming feelings of belonging. I knew these encounters were not going to happen often and that I would not get drawn in to the sex of it all but I did appreciate the insight to what happens when two women engage in playfulness such as we did. This is what comes natural to me, all the intimacy and enchantment that I got another peek at for one brief moment. Being with another woman is what defines not just my character but all that I am and who I am. It gave me cause to share the honest truth with my family.

I told my family I was changing jobs and working a different schedule which allowed me more time at home giving me longer week-ends. I was also looking forward to the increase in pay and hoping to be able save more money towards my own place or at least with a roommate. I would look up my friend Lisa Pascetti when the time came to see if she would be interested or consider sharing a place. I hadn't seen her in a while but talked to her every now and again. We keep in touch so that's helpful on my part. She is a cashier at Alpha Beta in San Marcos. The last weeks of work were used to gather personal information from those I wanted to stay in touch with.

I talked with Joni and hoped she would consider applying for at least one of the positions they have available for assembly. She took down the information and stuffed it in her wallet. I truly wanted her to come and work with me there because I know it would me a higher wage and she was an excellent worker who was comparably disciplined and loyal as I. I enjoyed being around her and would like to spend more time in her and her friends company when possible. She warned me about the consequences of being deeply involved with my girlfriend but I assured her that once I get established in my new job that I planned on moving on and ending our relationship all together.

Mom had informed me that she was alright with the arrangements of a new job and how anything that could improve my status was most helpful for everybody concerned. I was not opposed to helping out with things at home because Matthew participated as well and it wasn't just my obligation or responsibility. We did it because it was the right thing to do and just. I was looking forward to learning new things and meeting other people. My girlfriend wasn't too happy about it but understood. I didn't care for her reaction as I had felt she was getting much too possessive with my time and me.

She once said that she didn't care if I had boyfriends but she wouldn't tolerate other women! I thought that statement absurd under the circumstances but kept that to myself and thought that with this revelation out in the open it gave me the right to sever our relationship when the time came. I am not under obligation to anyone in this relationship or any other that may come. I took it all in stride after a few days of thinking about it and trusted that when the company made its move back down here to North County I could move on with my life and personal affairs.

I was to be there in the parking lot before sunrise for our forty five minutes to an hour caravan to work. I was introduced to the others on the van as well as those on the second van. Everyone was very friendly but went to sleep immediately after we entered the freeway exit and headed north. The traffic was light at first merging onto the Five Freeway as I stayed awake for the journey. I didn't pack a lunch for the first day as I was told there was a catering truck that came to the site three times a day and serviced other companies in the area. I was much too nervous to think about food that early to begin with.

Like I had done any other time in my life taking trains or busses to Los Angeles, I loved staring out the window and absorbing the sights around us even in the dark. I loved the miles of orange groves we passed once we got past the nuclear power plant. We had not yet expanded the freeways in either direction but it was in the very near future with the rate of people moving into the state. I was not looking forward to this migration of people because I knew that ultimately it would change the landscape of things all around and I just couldn't think that far ahead right now. The scenery was too beautiful to be interrupted.

I tried to live my life in a positive way and not allow the negative thoughts to invade my head. I would continue to see my therapist on Fridays and hope that I can come to some decision to share my dilemmas. I couldn't talk to her about the affair I was having and didn't want to lie about what type of relationship had developed. I despised my dad for all his adulteress affairs and now I was a part of one myself so I couldn't admit to being a bigot or want to admit it in fact. It didn't matter that I despised her husband for abusing her because she was a grown woman and should have been able to leave him.

He continued the abuse even while we conducted our affair and grew suspicious my presence anytime he was around. I never gave him any reason to think I was anything more then a friend when I was at their house with other friends and tried to keep my attention focused on others in the room whenever he was present. I do not comprehend what it is that brings a man to physically hurt a woman, their wives. I know it happens to many women and often for whatever reasons they cannot or will not leave them. I would do everything in my power to prevent or defend myself from anyone who threatened to bring harm to me or my sisters.

Mom on the other hand can defend herself as I have seen often in our lives. Many times she provokes and initiates the physical confrontations between her companions and I am most embarrassed by her behavior. I don't subscribe to the notion that one must use violence in order to maintain a healthy relationship or be in control of their partner. What is the point of controlling someone, especially someone you love or at least profess to love? I remember certain couples in high school who led secret abusive relationships and all I wanted to do was kick the shit out of the guy and slap the girl for allowing it. Abuse of any kind is not healthy.

It is unacceptable to me that couples whether their married or just dating show such little or no respect to their companions. Men especially are guilty of this behavior although mom is an exception and guilty on her part. We may be disappointed in one another but I have less respect for her in her behavior with her boyfriends whom she intimidates and or manipulates. I can't image why they allow her to treat them that way or tolerate such behavior from a woman. I may have many faults and may not be the best role model for my sisters but never could I cross the line of degrading someone I profess to love in the manner she does.

Sure she has issues with anger and alcohol, I have shared those same faults but never have I taken my aggressions out on anyone close whether it is child or companion. Our relationship will either be completely severed when I get around to telling her the honest truth about myself or she will for once think about someone other then herself and try to understand what it is I am saying. The scope of information I need to share with her will be enormous but not unbearable compared to how she's conducted herself over the years since the divorce.

She probably won't accept it or even like it but it is who I am and not what she had hoped I would be. I have tried to live my life for me and won't live out some expectation she saw in me. I'm running out of excuses and reason's to get on with my life if I don't have the support of my immediate family. Her rejection would not be a surprise but yet I would finally be able to say I gave this woman all I could in ways of sacrifices. I have no regrets about my responsibilities and self imposed obligations it was what I was taught and learned from having strong family traditions.

My new job was very different then what I came from but learning news things is good. The women are all quite friendly and the Spanish women are especially friendly as I struggled through my Spanish to tell them my name and a brief history of family. I explained my mother is Spanish and dad is Irish. They seemed to nod their heads in understanding but I couldn't realty tell. My lead lady Carol Snow was especially nice to me as she could tell how nervous I was in my silence and shyness during breaks and lunch. There was so much going on in my head that I really couldn't focus.

It was something I have struggled with lately because my personal life is in such dire straits. I didn't like being dishonest and there was a period in my life when I had become so lonely and distraught with not just my personal life but who I was as a humane being and I caused someone near and dear to me such pain that I lost them. What I did and the damage I caused her is unforgivable to me and that is something I will have to live for the rest of my life. I cannot begin to even forgive myself no matter what the reason it happened to begin with. I couldn't stop what was happening to me because I was like another person.

It is those regrets and not having a child while dating Mark that weight heavy on my heart and subjects that are a great source of writing material for my poetry. Thought they are my greatest source of unhappiness which follows me every day of my life being able to write poetry has brought some small amount of comfort to my aching heart. The first few days of work go surprisingly well and I am going to enjoy the short work week. It will allow me time to do some things around the house and spend an extra day with the dog. I have dropped out of my course in College and put it on the back burner for now although I continue to self study the course in my spare time.

Children and animals are my passion and anything I can do to help improve their lives or bring some measure of happiness and comfort to them is all the better for me. Life goes on and I am still able to play on both softball teams which is a great source of excitement and playful competition with friends and family. When my girlfriend asks me one day to leave my car with her as she has errands to run I have her drop me off at the van pool and she would pick me up afterwards. I wasn't opposed to doing that or even spending the night as I knew mom was growing highly suspicious of our friendship.

The weather in March was very wet and rainy and twice already I had missed the van pool and was forced to drive the route in horrible conditions. The people at work were giving me a hard time about my age insisting I could not possibly be twenty years old because I looked so much younger. I took it upon myself one day to bring in my birth certificate and show them how old I was, when and where I was born. They still found it hard to believe I was that age but looked so much younger. I attributed it to that child within who for so many reasons prevented me from being as mature as I know I should be.

I know I have behaved childishly on occasions when I should have taken a more mature approach to the situation but I cannot help that I am ultra sensitive about certain things and family issues. I am not a whole person and therefore am not grounded by any specific belief or conditions. Some subjects are completely off limits and I will not discuss or elaborate on any personal relationships. I am friendly otherwise to everybody and smile all the time but that facial reaction comes natural. I am friendly and enjoy greeting others with a smile because I like to see the same reaction when I meet people for the first time.

I acknowledge everybody with a smile because it's automatic. I have spent too much of my life alone without any expression because I'm busy thinking and it's not a healthy situation for me. Being idle has unfortunate if not dangerous consequences. I cannot afford to get depressed because I have the potential of doing great bodily harm to myself without thinking. If I expressed to anyone but my therapist how distressed I was for the most part I am certain she would do whatever she though necessary to have me committed for my own protection. I needed to tell her things that simply would not come out of my mouth.

I even thought about writing them down and giving them to her during our sessions but I couldn't even do that. I felt trapped and powerless and if something didn't change soon I would be forced to commit an act I have secretly wanted to do all of my life. Taking my own life was the easiest conclusion I knew of that would give me the peace I so wanted. When I arrived back to the parking lot that evening there was nobody there to pick me up and I was taken aback as to what to think. Others asked if I wanted a ride home and I thanked them but explained my ride was probably just running late.

Carol offered to wait until she arrived but I insisted she go home and I would call her when my ride showed up. I didn't want to over react so I walked over to Gemco and called her house. No sooner did I reach the payphone then I heard my car horn in the distance. I looked around until I spotted her and she pulled up to the curb with her friend Candy in the passenger seat. They had been out shopping and apologized profusely for not being there when the vans arrived. I glanced over at Candy briefly and said that was alright and proceeded to change seats with Candy as she went to the back of the car.

I was going to take that position as there was less room in the back of my fire-bird and she had longer legs then I but she insisted and I pulled my seat up a bit to give her more room. She invited, insisted I was staying for dinner and perhaps the night if I liked as we made our way down El Camino towards their house in the valley. I told her I needed to make a phone call soon as we arrived at the house to the woman who insisted on staying until she came because she was wor-ried. She inquired who the woman was and I said she was my lead. I didn't care for the tone in her voice but said nothing.

I called Carol immediately upon our arrival and told her I was home. She was celebrating the arrival of their adopted son and husband returning in just a cou-ple days but wanted to have some privacy with me before they arrived. I felt she was about to inform me that we could no longer continue with our affair but remain friends which would have been perfect. She would be the one to initiate the end and therefore would not be suffering any pain over the breakup. Candy stayed for dinner which consisted of very large porterhouse steaks, baked potatoe and collard greens. I loved the tastes of collard greens because it was so different from plain old spinach which I loved as well.

I learned to acquire a different more expanded taste of ethnic food while see-ing her and I appreciated the differences of taste to my mouth. Just like some people cannot stomach menudo I couldn't acquire a taste for liver! I walked Candy out to her car while my girlfriend attended to cleaning the kitchen. I kissed her on the lips and thanked her for being such a nice friend. I asked her for her phone number so I could keep in touch with her and she smiled as she pulled out a piece of paper and wrote her number. She looked at me inquisitively and leaned in to give me another kiss as I held open then closed her car door.

I had become very attracted to her and she knew it but nothing would possibly come of it. Although she experienced affairs with other women in the past and one relationship that lasted a few years her heart had been broken and she would not allow herself to be in that position again, ever. It was too bad for me but I was happy to know her and promised to stay in touch. My girlfriend came down the drive way presumably to find out what was taking me so long as I grabbed the garbage bag from her and took it to the trash at the side of the house. She asked what was taking so long and I explained we were talking about the baby.

She gave me that look of non-belief as she said it was time to go to bed since I had to be up so early to go to work. She thanked me for the use of my car and said she wanted to talk about something. I had prepared for her telling me we couldn't see each other like this any longer and explained why. There were some changes going to occur in her life that would require her full attention but that she still wanted me to be a part of her life. I was disappointed to hear those words come from her mouth but with a look of surprise I told her I would continue to come by and see her as I was able but couldn't promise anything definite.

She asked what that meant exactly and I told her I was thinking that now with her son coming and her husband getting out real soon it wasn't a good idea for me to risk spending any more time here then I use to. She looked at me with those sullen eyes and beautiful blonde hair and replied if I wasn't trying to say something I didn't want to admit. It was difficult for me to look into her blue eyes with dark eye liner and tell her I believed we had come to the end of our road so I explained that I wasn't going to beat around the bush. It would be best if we just called it a day but that I would come over or at least call first and see her when I could.

She piped up that since there was no commitment here and if I wanted to break off our affair she would understand but be very sad about it. I couldn't respond as we both retrieved to the bedroom to get ready for bed. If I learned anything in this relationship it is that being with a woman is what has been natural for me all along and I have no question of who I am or what my purpose in life is. We went to bed without any further conversation and watched television briefly before she fell asleep. The television would turn off automatically by eleven thirty news as I too feel asleep.

Come morning when the alarm went off she was not next to me and I could smell the aroma of coffee and food cooking. She said she couldn't sleep and didn't want to wake me so she was making me breakfast and prepared my lunch. It was a nice touch to end our affair but would manage to remain friends. I hugged her a long time after I took my shower and got dressed for work. I put my things in a brown paper bag making sure I didn't leave any incriminating evidence behind taking all my personal incidental effects and clothes I left here which she had put away when he was home.

Conversation was abrupt at breakfast as it was obvious this would be our last encounter here alone. I thanked her for breakfast and lunch and promised her I would be in touch but for her to call me when their son arrived. I promised to be there for her birthday party in a couple weeks where I could meet their son but I knew in my heart it would be the last time. I couldn't possibly remain friends with her after this and it was for the better on both accounts. I never cared for her husband for many reasons but his outward appearance lacked any semblance of decency.

He was a wife beater and therefore didn't rate any higher then dirt in my opinion. I didn't need to be associated with anyone who mistreated another humane being in that manner. I was better off getting on with my life but would always be eternally thankful for the things she expressed and shared with me on a more intimate level. Our encounters were far and few between but they gave me so much insight into myself and what I was truly all about. I could now look forward to the time when I would find someone suitable for me and develop a relationship that is hopefully meaningful and rich.

I have a renewed sense of self now and I can see my friends whom are in the same situation as me, not completely out to others much less themselves, and how they live their lives in secret. I can only hope this gives me the needed strength to tell my family, friends and therapist but we'll just have to wait and see taking one day at a time. At work there is this guy named Jeff McConkhill who has been overly friendly with me of late and has approached me on occasion to talk and share lunch with some afternoon. Carol tells me he is a very nice guy and she has known him many years.

They have worked their since the inception of the company and he will remain there even through the move in the next few months. I have driven by the building which is currently under renovation. Carol had moved down with her daughter when the employees were informed they were relocating to Carlsbad. Jeff lived at home with his parents and was unsure if he wanted to uproot his life and move down but would van pool in the meanwhile. He was a character straight out of Grizzly Adams, a mountain man who kept reminding me he was from Missouri, the show me state!

I found him quite refreshing and liked how he made me laugh. I was a bit shy around him because I had a feeling after talking with Carol that he had been inquiring of me and wanted to know if I had a boyfriend or not. I didn't want to mislead him in any way but I do enjoy his company and didn't mind spending my lunches with him. In the ensuing weeks and then into April when we were about to transition into the new building he invited me over to his house for lunch and perhaps meet his parents. I wasn't nervous but mostly excited because he had been gibing me a little family history and I was very interested in the Irish contents of each story.

I had become fond of Jeff because he was like a big cuddly bear with a full beard and mustache, shoulder length dark and a very hairy chest which sprouted out the top of his tee shirts or flannel shirts which he wore a lot of. The others in our little room of the building were teasing me about being his girlfriend but all I could do is smile and shake my head no, we are just very good friends and he is a very sweet guy but nothing else! I insisted it was all in their imaginations and that there was absolutely nothing going on or about to happen. I so wanted to tell them my attraction for women but didn't!

I could go along with the mischievous gossip that wasn't hurtful to either of us and just have fun. I'm sure mom would approve of him at first sight but that isn't likely to happen either. I'm not about to expose him to mom or anyone else in the family at the moment. He was pretty good-looking for a guy and full of energy and story. He was two years older then me and I had come to look forward to seeing him everyday. He has an older brother whom wants to be a priest and both parents seem very sweet. They live not far from work and so going to the house for lunch wasn't going to take any longer then our regular time allowed.

All the way there he told me the history of his neighborhood, the schools they attended as children growing up and what High School her graduated from. He had no real interest in College and wasn't sure what he was going to do yet. He asked me some things about myself and I shared all that I could. I have three older brothers, an older sister and two younger sisters. I did not however take any pleasure in telling him my parents were divorced or that my sister had runaway in her youth or any of the other unbearable truths of a shattered family in comparison to his life.

I only told him what I felt he could handle and not think that I was some unfortunate soul who needed rescuing from life's miserable peril. I do believe thought that if I was an ordinary girl like those in my family or like many of my straight friends that he could very well be a candidate for me to date. But my heart is not in it and I cannot succumb to head games or misleading myself as something I'm not. I do however like being around him and won't burst his bubble or perception of me. Nobody up here knows anything personal about me so I figure I'm safe and don't have to share any personal information that I don't want.

He lives in a well manicured neighborhood with many retired people scattered about and still others working for a living and raising a family. He shows me the house where an ex girlfriend lives and is still enamored with him but he wants nothing to do with her. It reminds me of where I came from to start out in happier days when I was but a child and had not lost my innocence. What would have become of me had William not taken my life in the way that he did? I do not dwell on that thought for more then a moment as I didn't want to miss anything Jeff was explaining.

We had a bologna sandwich with chips and a soda as we sat at the kitchen counter and he continued talking. There is some comfort in his company and I am feeling a bit sad that I have met him at a time when it has been revealed to me my own acceptance of being lesbian. I would not allow that impostor to ruin this guy's life because he is a rare find and a descent guy with real feelings and not a jerk like so many guys I grew up with and around. He was sincere and generally cared about so many things I cared about like the environment, over population and most especially the welfare of animals.

His parents had arrived just as we were leaving to return back to work and I extended my hand with an smile and greeted them with a; *hello and nice to meet you*. They made mention of what an unusual name I had and asked the origin if I didn't mind. I explained to them that at the time of my birth I was the fourth child of five to be born on the same exact date but not the same month and then I gave them the dates of my three brothers and one sister. I went further to elaborate how my sister really messed it up by arriving ten days earlier therefore putting a hiccup in the appropriateness of the name. However I had no complaints.

I don't think people see or share the same significance of the date as I do but that doesn't really matter, it is what it is and I can accept the facts for what they are. Nobody else has to know or think any different. On the way back to work we passed by his old girlfriends house where her parents were outside carrying groceries in from the car. Jeff tooted his horn to wave hello as they turned to wave back with their one empty hand. He made sure to drive slowly enough that they could see he had another girl in the truck with him. I leaned slightly in front of him so they could get a clear view and smiled.

He told me they had been disappointed in how their daughter mistreated him by dating a friend while she was seeing him for a few years. It's a shame that things like that happen all the time. I know the story and can relate to the pain it causes on many levels. You lose a certain amount of your trust for any other relationship that develops there afterwards and it's a shame that people can't be happy with what they have. In the ensuing weeks before our move down south I would join him at his parent's house on two other occasions and visit with his parents and meet his brother as well.

I was happy that they were moving because it was much closer to home and I would be spending all that wasted time on the road. I however would miss our Thursday evening stops at the local AM/PM where we gassed up and the company provided drinks of beer, wine or sodas with chips for the ride home. Only twice had we come in on a Friday either to make an order or pack up the area for the move. I had come to be a part of the family of this small company and looked forward to growing with them in the years to come. I had hoped to gain enough experience to transfer to the department that built the machines but for now it was a man's job exclusively.

I had gone to Carol's house on several occasions as well when she had invited me over for lunch and ended up cutting my hair or braiding it on occasions. She has a wonderful daughter in college but no husband and would not elaborate why. Carol is a tall heavy set woman much like my cousin Karla but much older. She lives in a wonderfully big house well decorated and beautiful gardens both front and back. My boss Terry Statzer had also relocated down here as was many of the upper management personnel. It is my understanding that these people have been long time friends and grew this company to what it is today and pretty much responsible for the success of it as well.

I was looking forward to whatever little contribution I could make as well. I was not at all anywhere as feminine as the other women who worked their but it was understood that none of the women could play ball the way I did and my capacity for sports would be unmatched by many of the guys as well. They had a team that played whenever they had their company picnic and the company had a men's team there in Santa Ana. Jeff was impressed and didn't seem to mind my tomboyish characteristics. Not that it would have made any difference because it's the simple nature of who I am.

He's never seen a woman quite like me who excelled and most of the time surpassed the skills of a lot of the guys on the team and other teams he's played against. I take great pride in my abilities and skills as an athlete first before being a woman. I expressed to him that when he comes down sometime he should stay long enough and watch my team play. He said he would do that and gladly accepted the invitation. It was time for the company to move into its new headquarters and he would be a part of the crew that set up the stockroom which is where he worked.

I had not bragged about him to mom or the girls because I didn't want to get their hopes up or give them any inclination to read something into our friendship other then us just being that, friends. I mentioned him as among the other people I had befriended and that was fine. It was going to be moms birthday soon and I thought it would be nice to get her a piano since it is something she mentioned she's like to own some day. Aunt Stella and Dora both have one that little David gets his lessons on and he play's quite well I understand. So does Aunt Stella's youngest son Richard.

David is exceptional and can play anything from classical to contemporary. He has been playing from an early age and his father is very strict in what he plays not allowing him the freedoms to express his abilities or choices of music. The point is that he's concert quality and one day he's going to make his living at that passion. If I had the talents that he possess I would pursue them vigorously. I always loved babysitting for him and his sister Sonia when they were little because they were such well behaved kids, quiet and more reserved then any relative of the entire family.

They were so much different then Williams children who could fill a stadium with the energy and enthusiasms they exhibited when I babysat them. What a joy they were each and every time I had the pleasure of taking care of them. They have wildness about them I could relate to and can remember having in the beginning of my life when we kids were altogether. Week-ends at Grandmothers was an event filled with fond memories and deep creased smiles that I look back on any time I'm around joyful kids. We don't have those kinds of get tog ethers anymore except at funerals or weddings.

I was disappointed not to be able to attend Karla and Norms wedding this week-end, April twenty second because I will be out of town at a softball tournament in Palm Springs. I know mom and the girls will be there so I can make my inquiries with them and hopefully see some pictures later on. I'm hoping mom or someone will save me a piece of cake. They have been dating for sometime now and it was a good thing that their going to finally get married. Karla and Kammillie are the same age practically just a hours a part but to me it's close enough for them to be the same age.

I don't know if Kammillie will make it down for the wedding since she doesn't participate in family events any longer unless it's stuff with dad and *that* part of the family. I decided to check out the prices of an upright at Greens Pianos in Escondido for the best selection. I had no idea what I was looking for but I did know how much I was ailing to pay. I would use my income taxed for thee down payment and make monthly installments. I choose a mahogany upright with the most beautiful rose engravings throughout and settled in for the paperwork which would take at least the next hour.

I discussed this with the girls who thought it might be a good idea as well. I don't like spending money excessively but I was just trying to establish some credit for when I wanted to buy a mobile home which many of my friends said was a good alternative to a house. On my Carlsbad softball team I come to find out there are two gay couples that are not out but others know about. People don't make such a big deal about their relationship basically because it's nobody's business and they aren't any different around other women on the team or opposing teams. I'm finding out that there are quite a number of gay women in both leagues!

I have called my friend a few times since her birthday and since the baby and her husband came back. They were doing quite well considering and she asked when I would be stopping by. I told her I would most likely be able to stop at his baseball game at Landis park one evening but not able to go to the house since I would not feel comfortable. I didn't want to provoke him into accusing her of anything by me being there so its better off I leave well enough alone. I missed her but I've learned to move on. I haven't had the guts to share that with my therapist either but I'm still trying to work up the nerve to tell her I'm gay.

Our tournament in the desert proved to be high ranking even thought we didn't win it but placed high in the rankings. It is a formidable group of women who seem to have the best of times and are highly spirited. There are those teams whose attitude appears to be more of a professional manner than just going out and playing to the best of one's ability. We aren't cut throat or don't try to play so aggressively that it takes away from the sportsmanship of the game. Our team in Oceanside, the Cerda Brothers is more of an ensemble of clowns then athletes because although we play well together Colleen and I are sometimes at odds with one another.

It's a team different then my Breakers but enjoyable none the less. We play in a lower league then Carlsbad but have just as much fun. Mom will come to our games as often as she can and sits with her friends and there is not a game that goes by that our dear friend Mary Martinez does not attend. Her daughter Linda plays on it as well. She married her high school sweetheart and mutual friend David Atoe. We have a couple of high school sweethearts in our class that got married after high school like Becky DiPietro and Ron Johnson and the class ahead of us Linda Penning and Pete Wesloh, Carol Viera and Anthony Paopao just to name a few.

The piano would be delivered the week-end of her birthday and I managed to get Aunt Stella to agree to have her out of the house for the better part of the morning into early afternoon when the delivery had been scheduled by noon. I just needed a few hours cushion just in case there were unexpected complications. Everyone was excited and managed to keep their secret the whole while. I didn't want to move any furniture or rearrange anything while mom was home to give away the surprise. She and I may not get along and we certainly have our differences but it doesn't mean she doesn't deserve nice things.

I will always be thankful to her for managing to keep all seven of us children after dad left as opposed to giving us up or other alternatives. I know how hard it was to raise us on her own without any financial assistance of a job other then child support. I suppose she did the best she could under the circumstances. Being on welfare was a disgrace in itself but she had absolutely no other choices. I would not let myself get in this type of situation ever in my life and so marrying a man will never happen. I often thought about that prospect in high school with Mark to have a child, get married and lead our separate lives but that failed as well.

It was a doable concept but you needed both parties to participate and his mother saw to it that never happened. It was heart wrenching not to have gotten pregnant during our thirteen months together when I tried like hell no matter how unnatural it was for me. I would have made any sacrifice necessary needed to get pregnant and failing to do so after so long nearly disabled me emotionally. I had to wonder just what it was I had done that caused God to turn away from me like He had. The sins I committed, lies I told and pain I caused others could be easily explained but I was clueless to the severity of my crimes against Him.

Nobody knows our relationship and therefore is easily critical of me and my actions. I am already prepared for the onslaught of rejection and hurtful words that will spill out of the mouths of those who profess to love me. My kind are not looked upon kindly no matter how we have conducted our lives aside of the sexual issues. It is nobody's business what your private life consists of when you're an adult and in the privacy of your own home. You can be a prostitute, drug dealer, thief, wife beater, child abuser, child molester but if you are a homosexual you are deemed a criminal against humane nature.

How can I defend myself against a society who judges me in that manner? I remember as a four and five year old child watching all the horrific news about Blacks fighting for civil rights in the sixties and how the ignorance, anger and fear caused certain people to act ungodly. Yet for the most part in time attitudes began to change and those who so vigorously opposed Blacks from getting an education, eating in the same establishments amongst white patrons and dating their sons and daughters started to changed. That's not to say there still aren't those people out there who are determined to keep that separation and war alive.

Change is always dangerous in a society who is use to traditional family values of an ordinary kind. Humane nature cannot be altered by those who both oppose it and disapprove of it. I know it is ultimately my responsibility to educate my family about who I am and do every thing I can to dispel their fears. I want to enlighten them to the goodness in me and not see me as a sexual deviant. I am their sister, daughter, cousin, Aunt and even teacher because who I am will have to be explained in terms that they can comprehend. I cannot speak for the millions of other lesbians in the world but I can share the essence of me.

If I cannot be honest with myself how can I possibly portray to my family the positive attributes I possess? I have to say that I believe my childhood friends and Mr. and Mrs. Kaahaaina may possibly be more receptive and accepting of me then my own family. I have to ask; *am I willing to be estranged from my family who means so much to me at the cost of setting me free?* As often as I say; *I am totally aware of the consequences I face,* will I really be able to move on and live a meaningful and productive life? At what point does a person stop sacrificing their own existence for their family?

It's a perfect topic in my next session of therapy but sharing it may be another battle. I have envelopes containing lists of subjects to share with her but I don't ever bring them out when I'm there. Instead they remain folded in the back pocket of my Levis or locked in the glove compartment of my car. That little girl in me reminds me with each session that the wound is to big to be repaired. How can I heal if I'm unable to bring myself to talk about it? My conversations with God my Father are long winded and emotional but He offers no visible solutions that I am aware for which I can overcome these secrets.

I am twenty years old, responsible, self sufficient and live up to my family obligations but I cannot manage to get away from the torment I live each and every day. I surround myself with friends and positive people yet I am helpless to standup on my feet and declare my truth. Who will suffer the most by my silence but me? Once the piano arrives and we manage to get it put in it's proper place against the wall behind the front door Aunt Stella drives up shortly afterwards just as the delivery truck has made it's u-turn at the end of the street. Mom didn't even notice the truck but looked surprised at so many people loitering in the living room.

Before she could finish her question as to why she turned to see the piano and was overwhelmed with emotion. We all smiled and gathered around her as she pulled out the bench and sat down lifting up the keyboard cover. She ran her hands against the face of the upright feeling the texture of the designs. We sang happy birthday in unison as everyone smiled and watched her caress the keys. She pressed down softly on the keys in no particular order or fashion but made wonderful noise. She mentioned it needed to be tuned and I told her there was a guy coming out next week-end.

It was perhaps the second single most inspiring thing I could have done for her besides her puppy last year. I just wanted her to be happy and to know we really do appreciate her for so many reasons even if we don't often tell her. There was no hidden motive here, just a gift from all of us in thanks for all that she has done and continues to do. We can never forget her struggles along the way but also she hopefully will embrace ours as well. Richard and little David sat down as mom encouraged David to play something, anything he wanted and there he sat expressing himself playing a Beatles tune.

It was a birthday she would not forget anytime soon and no matter what our differences she will always be my mother. I was off to play ball but would return later to go out for pizza at Filippi's downtown. Softball has always been a lifesaver for me because my friends bring so much joy to my life. The whole idea of hitting the ball harder and farther then the competition was effortless for many of us. Playing with girls of the same caliber made the game more competitive. It's what makes me happy. I set aside the inner issues of discontent for the remainder of the day to enjoy my family.

As we try to get moved in to our new building at work Jeff has approached me for a date and I finally give in because how hard could it be? The company is sponsoring a day at the stadium to watch the Angels and Padres. I of course will be rooting for the Angels because I like certain players and the company is from that area so I just want to offer my support. He would drive down early and pick me up in the morning for breakfast and we would head to the stadium from there. We would meet others at the tailgating event before the game to get ourselves all fired up! I was looking forward to the game and all the fun which came with it.

I was hesitant about bringing him inside to meet the family and took extra precautions to make sure the house was as clean and straightened up as possible. I was not happy that he was so anxious to meet mom and the rest of the family. But there was nothing I could do to avoid or dissuade him. I suggested without success meeting me at work with those who are taking the bus down. I suppose since I had met his parents and brother now it's his turn to meet mine, *oh joy* I thought to myself. It was early in the season and the first of many trips they have planned for the year. I was looking forward to spending some play time with these people to get to know them better.

I prepared the family for meeting Jeff and told them a little about him just to ease their minds and they seemed receptive but I did notice a little gleam of curiosity in mom's eyes. I assured her; *he is just a friend and don't expect anything to come out of it because she will be sorely disappointed.* It would be a mistake for her to presume otherwise. There have been others that she has tried to encourage me to see but I wouldn't have it. There was always something I was doing or someplace I was going. No time for men and certainly no blind dates. I was not going to have her try and influence who I saw or where I went.

My sisters had no choice because they were under eighteen but Matthew and I were older and would be able to move out if we so chose. When Jeff showed up I hesitantly let him in the house which I spent a better part late into the night cleaning. The dog was the first to approach him and proceeded to shove his nose into his crotch where he quickly leaned down and diverted her attention to his hand while he patted the top of her head gently. He said that was alright and that he was use to dogs doing that because it was better then smelling his butt as they do with one another.

Everyone else was cordial as was Matthew upon exiting the bathroom and extended his hand in greetings. Jeff quickly excused himself to use the bathroom when the girls and mom both turned to me complementing how handsome and courteous he was. I agreed that *yes* he was a perfect gentleman but most of all a very nice guy and a lot of fun to be around. Matthew was on his way to David's house to finish some picture he was doing for him and left promptly. David had acquired quite an extensive library of his drawings and encouraged Matthew to pursue a career in it.

Matthew has been dealing with some issues of a more personal nature and unable to deal with anything that required any seriousness. The girls sat on the couch across from mom who was waiting patiently for Jeff to return to view. I could see that they had those inquiring looks and wanted to question him some but I told them we had to go because we would be meeting others in the stadium parking lot after breakfast. I didn't give them the slightest opportunity to find out anything more then they needed aside from his name and where we were going. He seemed uncomfortable that I was hurrying him along but time was a wasting I told him.

I ushered him toward the front door as he turned and made mention of what a beautiful piano that was. I told him it was a birthday present for mom just a week or so ago and he wanted me to expand on the answer but I insisted we should leave and off we went. We waved good bye and he called out; *it was nice to meet you hope to see you again.* It may have appeared rude on my part but I insisted they had the ability to talk his socks off and I wanted out of there. We talked mostly about me and my life when we sat for breakfast at the diner on El Cajon Boulevard. I was only willing to submit a specific amount of information nothing deeply personal.

I liked him a lot but I neither wanted to lead him on nor scare him off. I seemed to be in conflict with my inner child of late which was a subject I brought up in therapy. We took our time during breakfast and I thanked him for the meal. Once we arrived at the stadium and found the rest of our company we joined them and I could just see the inquiring minds hard at work. I had grown use to those stares by now and as much as they were harmless there was also hope from a select few that we would become an item. I would not give them cause or confirm any rumors that we were anything but friends.

People knew him well but they didn't know me and I was not about to show them any false hopes. We sat for a short while before we were to pack up and head to the stadium as others began trickling in to join us. It was a beautiful Saturday afternoon and I looked forward to the goings on with this new found family I've joined. We are slowly settling in at work but there still needs lots of finishing off to do. The crowd looked evenly scattered as Padre fans displayed their versions of team uniforms while Angel fans wore their infamous traveling uniformed colors, red on white.

For the ensuing four or so hours we cheered the Angels with every exciting play and successful hit and by the conclusion of the ninth inning the Angels had managed to stay ahead of the game by two runs giving them the victory in the end. People were surprised at my cheering for their team since I was a native but I assured them I was not a fan of either sports home team. I grew up following the Cincinnati Reds and Pittsburg Steelers. I really had no loyalties to anything outside of God and my family. I had a thoroughly good time and thanked Jeff for being such a good sport when I ushered him through meeting my family.

At the end of the day after he dropped me off at home I said my goodbyes and waved him off. I could see the curious faces peering through the sheer curtains on the front door window as I reach for the handle. Before any of them could speck I assured them with a serious tone that he is not my boyfriend and don't go expecting me to go out on another date with him. We are co-workers and that's all there is to the story, the end! I wanted no discussion or debate about him and they realized this when I went in the bedroom. The girls said mom had gone out dancing and would be home a little later but not past midnight.

I never knew when she was going to have Andreas stay over so I just claimed the couch as my place to sleep. It had been a long day and I was exhausted but I had a lot of fun. I was sorry if they had expected anything more from me but I have my own agenda and he just isn't part of it. Yes he is a very rare guy, sweet guy, even a great guy but I'm not the one for him. I would only end up hurting him and I cannot do that. For Mothers Day there is a big family gathering at Mission Bay where everyone is expected to show up and I am looking forward to seeing all the kids once again.

It has been far to long since our last gathering aside from Karla and Norms wedding but not all the family showed up for that so this would be a treat for me. In therapy I expressed the dilemma I was in with my inner child and we took steps to reconcile the issue. I had hoped to prompt her to inquire further with some leading questions which would force me to bring up the sins of my past but it's not what happened. She didn't probe as deeply as I expected her and therefore I was left out on a limb. It is this area specifically that I wish she would be more aggressive, more assertive with me but she's not.

There are times in therapy when I need her to lead me down a path I have resisted. I do not have the inner strength to carry this up from the dungeon myself and require some prodding but how does a patient go about inspiring her therapist to use more aggressive approach then what she's offering? If she can't help me get it out then I'm in worse trouble then when I first came in. The picnic was turning out to be the biggest family affair in years. Everyone brought all sorts of dishes from meats and salads to fruits and veggie platters. Naturally the guys bought plenty of beer and a couple bottles of wine while enough sodas were available for everyone.

The cake was a two part full sheet cake with the entire list of mother's name on it. There was volleyball set up and later on there would be mush ball to play. It was a day which brought back the fondest of memories of times long ago. Everyone form Aunt Connie's three kids and nine grandchildren to Aunt Stella's crew, Aunt Josephine and Uncle Manuel's group, to Uncle Robert and Aunt Mila's kids. It was a beautiful day and the bay was crowded with hundreds of people celebrating the mom's of the family. It was so nice to see everybody in one place and we all had a great time. Mike and Charlotte where here with their two sons but his brother Mark was not.

For the entire time we were together there was non stop playing, eating and drinking of all sorts. I loved to hear the laughter of children as the kids played near the grandmas of the family. I hung out with Cecilia, Betty, Lucy and Karla for a while until the games began. First there were three games of volleyball that took the better part of the morning through lunch. When it appeared that we had tired out all the children and mot of the teenagers we started up the game of mush ball. Every adult who was able and wanted joined in the fun and we had the time of our lives.

Some of our Aunts joined in just to show up their husbands who didn't want any part of it except Uncle Robert who pitched a few times for the men. It reminded me of the importance of family and how alone you can be without them. No matter what one's transgressions or faults there is still family to come home to and I had to wonder if that was true for me. There are plenty of guilty parties in this crowd of one offense or the other but for someone to stand up and declare their sexuality was simply not going to be accepted. Aunt Rose and Michael are here but Johnny was not and I had depended on him for moral support.

He is two years younger then me but his confidence has led him to be open about his sexuality and nobody in the family has neither disputed nor discussed it. If I had half his self esteem I might have been a different person earlier instead of continuing to struggle. It wasn't a part of family gatherings to include Johnny so I couldn't find out what it was like for him to be living as a young gay guy. I was looking forward to some enlightenment, some personal insight into our world but that wasn't going to happen today. I know the best thing for me to do was just drive down here and spend some time with him.

I didn't feel comfortable approaching Aunt Rose in front of all the relatives she was congregated around so I left that alone as well. I would have to find other avenues of gathering my information under different means. The only thing I could do is leave word with Aunt Rose that I would like to come down and spend the day with her and Johnny. I needed to put every effort possible to pursuing this matter and learn from their relationship. She is the closet to mom out of all her sisters and being an ex nun might be what mom needs to understand that I am no different a daughter because my reality is non traditional.

I cannot change their way of thinking if they don't allow me to be open and honest. As it nears the time that people are beginning to pack up and leave I do what I can in any way to help them and carry things to their cars, help with gathering the children and cleaning up after ourselves. I am thankful for the love this family ultimately shows for one another. I can only hope that they will continue to feel that way when yet another family member comes out and declares their rightful place within the family. Love is a powerful word and I have to believe that it is never ending where family is concerned.

For the remainder of the month through June and now into July we are about to come upon another birthday in the family with Colleen, her sweet sixteenth. Jeff and I had not gone to the ball games together but instead met on the bus and went from there along with the other employees who went. I continued to be friends and behave as thought nothing had changed because it hadn't. He realizes that I am not going to be a part of his life in the way he had hoped and others finally accepted that as well. There was however a different guy at work who was actually one of the men working construction there who expressed his interest in me as well.

He left me his phone number and pleaded on many occasions for me to call him. I had spoken to him a few times and had admired his physique. As a lesbian I admired the toned body no matter whom it was attached to. Whether it was a construction worker or a woman athlete and I have had the pleasure on many occasions to be in the same company as very well built, fine tuned women athletes with great shapes. For years I've been working out with free weights and keeping fit otherwise but I don't have the sculpted body I'd like with cut abs and chiseled upper body muscles. My legs need extensive toning and running gives me wrestler's legs, thick and manly looking.

I don't want to look like a man but I am in pursuit of a better conditioned and toned body. I've lost the extra saddle bags I had gathered last summer and my gut is nearly flat once again but my worst enemy is the hip area which is well cushioned. I may have a great waist but my big hips distort my other wise shapely figure. I use Matthews's weights for now but eventually I will purchase a set of my own. With Colleen's birthday just around the corner I ask her what she would like that mom can't necessarily afford but that I might pitch in and help her. She would like a boom box, a very specific, very expensive model and I tell her I'll see what we can do.

It is with great concern that I wonder what prompts some people to be so different then others in the same family. I admire Colleen's ability to be so opinionated and not hold anything back but also disapprove of her constant need of things as thought she is owed this stuff. She doesn't ever say; *I would like to* or *it would be nice to have this or that.* She requests things that she is certain she will get without question or hesitation. She believes with the utmost certainty that everything she says she wants she is by all means going to receive it! I couldn't be so bold and nobody else in the family ever has had that attitude.

I discussed the options with mom who elaborated that Colleen had been doing so well in school and was on track with her grades, one compliment after the other, that she deserved whatever it was she asked for. I was flabbergasted to say the least because even though I displayed these same enthusiasms and ambitions way earlier then she did and many times my request were at no cost to her, she denied me each and every time. How absurd I thought to myself and it was no wonder that Michelle felt the way she did. Mom catered to Colleen in ways I was embarrassed and disgusted.

She has two daughters living at home and by her comments it was obvious to me she had shunned the youngest. I don't know what went on here while I was away for that year but I can tell it was not good for Michelle. Colleen has had her share of difficulties but mom was always there to support and defend her yet on the other hand when it came to Michelle or I we were practically invisible. I can see why Michelle has revolted in the ways she does. She gets no quality of attention from mom except to be disciplined or chastised for one reason or another. I fear she will end up resenting mom as deeply as I do but what to do?

In mid July I am told by a friend about a good job that was coming up at the facility where she worked and that I should apply. It was a place called *Singer/Kearfott* in San Marcos across from the High School and they worked government jobs paying good money and had a union. I had only been on this job nearly six months and we just moved down here, I wasn't sure I could leave them so soon. I had managed to get my former girlfriend a job here as well and things were working out good for her. The family was coming along and her husband wasn't beating her on a regular basis.

Now that they had a child to raise I was hoping he would be a better person but one never knows like with cats that can't change their stripes. Softball was going good and we were playing a lot of tournaments. I was no longer being pursued by the construction worker and Colleen was dating this guy off and on which kept her off Michelle's back. Mom was still dating Andreas and sometimes their relationship turned physical where she would make his life miserable if they had too much to drink and came home to drink even more. Mom has had a real problem with excessive drinking and I had wished she would back off some.

Colleen got her very expensive boom box and I was determined to make it up to Michelle come Christmas. It was not like me to behave in that manner but what mom was doing was wrong and it was bad enough she treated me that way, I wasn't going to allow Michelle to suffer because of it. With a bit of guilt and reluctance I applied for that job and after many interviews with a host of people and one session of grueling questions as to why I was willing to leave a perfectly good job and come there I simply stated the opportunity seemed better. In August I would begin my new job after having given two weeks notice with Eaton/Leonard.

I expressed my wishes to return back to school and get my teaching credentials and work nights. They were totally supportive and understanding. They gave me a very nice pen set at my departure and some company memorabilia and invited me to join them anytime at the company sponsored events. I promised to keep in touch and left after the two weeks. It was a difficult decision at first because I was unsure if I was going to be able to get in. Singer had a reputation for being tough to get into but when the call came and I passed all the tests including the soldering test which was limited because I was to be a mechanical assembler and they don't solder, I took it.

My first day on the job I was to sit in a class with twelve other new hires and one or two people I recognized from previous jobs at ACDC. It is a big facility with over four hundred people working three shifts. I would be in this class all week until Friday morning when the department Supervisor would come get me. In the meanwhile I was assigned a job in the printed circuit board department until my mechanical assembly job opened up. I started out on first shift for the first month then went to second the end of September. I was excited about this job for many reasons.

I was excited for both as Colleen this year, marks the beginning of the end of a family tradition with our family attending Oceanside High School. Colleen is a senior and will graduate next June while Michelle is a freshmen and the last of the Kelly family to go through this district. All seven of us kids even Matthew started out here until his junior year, transferred to and graduated from Monte Vista in Spring Valley. He was the first boy of the three to graduate while I was the first so far of the girls. Both Clifford and Kammillie dropped out of high school and Kristopher was killed in a car accident in his sophomore year.

I would still be able to continue with my therapy and I got a more then fifty cent pay raise. The potential for making a lot more money was greater in this job which meant I could save more and get my own place. The best part was they have an automatic plant shut down for one week paid holiday vacation at Christmas. Things at home were changing as well as in my life. There was this friend of Andreas's who wanted to meet me but I wasn't interested. He was a tall, thin Mexican guy with dark mysterious eyes and dark mustache who would come here after work and talk with the others on the crew which Andreas was a part of.

They are cement workers and his boss really likes the work he does. His name is Fernando Olazabo and he's just twenty two years old. He doesn't have any family here because he's from Mexico. He has seen me on many occasions but I never noticed him before and he spoke less English then Andreas. October was one of my favorite months of the year because if the humongous size of the moon. It's what people call a harvest moon and when it's full it looks as thought you can just reach out and touch it. It lights up the night like nothing I've ever seen any other month of the year not even with a new moon.

I had become a very busy person not just on the job but in my personal life as well. Fernando expressed an interest in dating me and I was being hounded by mom to go out with him. I didn't need or appreciate the intrusion but gave in eventually because so many things at home have changed recently. Matthew was having serious mental issues from years of drug abuse and it looks as though mom may have to hospitalize him for his own safety. He wasn't hurting anybody but the dog every now and again when Matt would kick him out of anger or frustration. He was becoming unpredictable with his moods and fighting constantly with mom.

There was family turmoil and I couldn't make things worse by announcing I was a lesbian and I wanted everyone to know it! Although I felt my time was running out and I was about to lose my identity forever and return back to the dungeon of my soul, I spoke to Fernando and tried with great difficulty to communicate. Michelle was helpful as she tagged along when we went some place to pick up dinner and bring it home. Michelle spoke better Spanish then I because all her girlfriends are Mexican and their teaching her the language which she's picked up fairly easily. I have no excuse and appreciated her support.

I wasn't at all happy about this situation and I don't know what's going to come of it but right now my lesbianism will have to wait. With the situation concerning Matthew growing increasingly unstable mom makes a few phone calls and speaks to our therapist to find out what she can do. I can see how she is tormented by her decision but for Matthews's sake something has to be done. He's soon to be twenty two years old and something is desperately wrong with him. Before Thanksgiving holiday she takes Matthew down to San Diego to a facility for evaluation that will be able to help him.

I stay home with the girls while Aunt Stella accompanies her and she will remain in San Diego all week-end staying with Aunt Josephine. I do my best to explain to Colleen and Michelle that Matthew was in trouble and he needed some help so mom took him to a hospital where he could get that type of treatment. They asked if he went to the crazy house and I told them; *absolutely not!* He is not crazy, just a little mixed up. It is something that happened as a result of Kris's death over eight years ago. Everybody deals with loss in their own way and apparently Matthew has suffered pain that nobody was aware of.

I miss Kristopher and I was sorry they didn't know him like we did, they would have liked him. Matthew was not a lost cause but he did need immediate attention and mom had to deal with that situation in her own way. It was best she stayed in San Diego for the time being. Thanksgiving will be a bit more difficult this time around and we are invited to San Diego where I will join everybody after our tournament. I have Michelle come with me to assure mom we will be back before dinner. Work is good and I am happy I took the job even though I miss my friends from Eaton/Leonard.

There is a guy here I used to work with at ACDC, Mike Cooper from the stockroom, Becky Cerda whom I played ball with on her husbands team and mom's friend Teresa. It is a big place and some people I recognize but haven't approached yet because our breaks are different. The big boss Larry Caterino makes his presence every hour just so we don't get carried away with our conversations. He is from the plant in New Jersey and is now Manufacturing Plant Manager. He's a big Italian guy who looks like a typical Mafioso character you see in all the Italian mafia movies.

Our tournament went well and we placed in the top three so we improved with every game which made the coach happy. It was a round robin and we have been playing since eight thirty this morning. I called mom and told her we were on our way. She said there was plenty of time since dinner wouldn't be ready for another two hours or so. I was glad we had been invited down here for many reasons. We always played in the Thanksgiving Day tournaments and I couldn't not play. Michelle met all my closet teammates and I told her that some of those women were gay bu5t didn't point them out specifically to see what her reaction would be.

She seemed surprised since she didn't know any real ones personally. It was hopeful and I though to myself that I would tell her first before mom whenever it was I decided to come out. I was looking forward to Johnny being there so I could try and talk to him. I called to make sure there wasn't anything I could stop at the grocery store and pick up but they said everything was all set. The street was almost filled to capacity with cars lined on both sides but there was a few spots open near the end of street by their house so I pulled in there. I recognized most of the cars and when we got inside the house was filled with relatives.

Even the newlyweds were there as well. Kammillie never called or showed up but I guess that wasn't a disappointment as we've grown accustomed to her saying one thing and not following through. I would love to just once be all together with everyone and their children, just once. The weather was pretty outside but cool. Everyone was in their little groups talking about whatever subject was at hand. The kids were in the backroom playing games while the teenagers were out in the backyard congregated around the patio table. I hadn't spotted Johnny yet but Aunt Rose and Mike were there.

It was a day spent visiting and talking about times long past and of course eating. There were two turkeys and lots of fixings. Johnny never did show up, previous commitments I understand so once gain I'm going to have to wait. We stayed until early evening after everyone was given a little care package. Mom didn't appear as jovial as usual during these feasts but I guess Matthew was heavy on her mind. It would be at least a month or two before we could go visit him because he was currently under observation and they wanted absolutely no family contact.

I know it's going to be difficult but she will have to manage some how. I asked her on the drive home if I could clean out the garage and fix it up a little better to make it into my own room in his absence. She said it would be alright but to make sure and pack his things so we could bring his art supplies to him when he's better and able to have them. We didn't know how long he was going to be in that place and they didn't give mom and clear answer either. I can image it brought back difficult memories for her when dad, Louie and William forcibly removed her from our house that summer afternoon when I was younger and took her to a facility down in the valley.

It was not a happy time for any of us. When you're that young there is so much you cannot comprehend and what you see can be very disturbing to you. By the time we got home and put everything away I gave mom the newspaper so she could go through it. I would read the paper every now and again but didn't make a ritual of it. I preferred reading and writing when a thought provoked me. I was half heartedly looking forward to Christmas this year and with Matthew's absence mom was anxious to see when we could visit him. Although we returned to work and the girls back to school mom was obviously stressed over the situation.

I don't know if she had any contact with dad about what was going on and I didn't care to ask. When I returned to work people were asking if I had seen the newspaper article in the Blade Tribune. The story is about me and two others from our department who were recognized for our United Way/Chad contributions. There was a picture of me, Lee Maglietto and Regina Daggett our lead lady with our company campaign chairman Courtland Frye. I saw the paper and believe mom went through it but said nothing to me. They had a copy of it in the lab area and I would see it soon as I got a break.

It has always been something I feel very good about being able to give to charities of my choice. It's simple when it comes directly out of your paycheck and you really don't miss it. I give the most I am able to two different charities; Canine Companions for the disabled and a Children's charity. I'm very passionate about supporting causes dear to my heart and soul and both these qualify for that. I will be a loyal contributor for as long as I'm employed here. I have joined the ranks of another charity in donating blood. My family has been devastated by cancer of all sorts and the least I can do is donate something we all should be doing as we're able.

I believe in giving back to your community or at least contributing to whatever cause is true to your heart. I was happy with the picture since it captured me at my desired weight which was something I struggled with when I returned last year. My appearance is a big factor in how I see myself as a person and what I want to portray. I live on a very emotional rollercoaster which dictates most of my habits from eating to socialization. It looks as though I will be staying in this department until after the New Year when the Mechanical assembly job will be available first week of January.

Mom was still feeling pretty sad over the issues with Matthew and although the family was trying to carry on as best we could it was not quite the same. I had asked Michelle to assist me in talking to Fernando about fixing up the garage so I could make it into my room temporarily. It took about two week-ends to clean up Matthews's portion, put his things in a box and store them in the garage then figure out how I wanted the room. I would buy a twin bed and mattresses, desk for my writing and a dresser for the little bit of clothes I had. I'm not like my sisters or ordinary girls who have massive amounts of clothes of various style and color.

I'm very simple in my wardrobe; Levis, tee shirts, underclothes of course and tennis shoes. I don't wear fancy clothes or own a dress, which would be way out of character for me. Even though I wore them in high school at Mark's request they were mom's dresses. The slacks I own are packed away under protective plastic. It would have to somehow be insulated because it gets cold out there in the winter time which is now upon us. We go through the ritual of buying a live Christmas tree and decorating it even when mom suggested we just put up the fake one. I don't think so and off the girls and I went.

We did the best we could to brighten up the house with decorations and make it as festive as possible under the circumstances. I know mom didn't feel very Christmassy but she would have to manage to get through it. She went back to therapy shortly before taking Matthew to San Diego and remains going to her sessions now. All of us, except Michelle, go and I think it would be a good idea if she went once a month herself. The family sessions would never work with this foursome but I believe it's helping that those of us who do participate are making an effort to get better. Michelle didn't feel she had anything to contribute or wanted to share.

I bought the girls a few items they requested like specific clothes, shoes and school supplies. Colleen had become an avid sewer and was doing pretty good making some of her own blouses. I still have the shirt she made me for my sixteenth birthday which I cherish dearly. Through as much turmoil as our relationship has suffered she can manage to do some nice things for me once in a while. We bought mom some perfume, jewelry and her favorite box of Whitman's sampler chocolates. She doesn't seem to be impressed with the See's brand, says it's over priced but the rest of us like it none the less.

There was a shadow of sadness Christmas morning at Matthews's absence and so I passed out the gifts to everyone and Andreas gave all of us a little something himself. He wasn't a replacement for a male figure in the family but he was the only one available. We would go down to see Matthew later in the afternoon for a short visit because it's all they allowed. If it wasn't for the holiday we wouldn't be able to see him at all. As it is only mom is allowed to visit with him for reasons unknown to me and she isn't talking. I bought myself the furniture for the room we made in the garage and mom gave me writing materials.

We got phone calls from relatives and spent the day quietly at home having a nice dinner. The girls and I cooked a ham and all the trimming giving mom a much needed break. She spent the day with Andreas who took her to San Diego to see Matthew. The week off from work I spend organizing the room as I wanted it and played with the girls and the dog. I have Laddie sleep with me at night to help keep me warm and I know he loves that since it beats the cold ground. Mom doesn't particularly care for it but it is what it is. He's not just a dog to me but a companion and I'll treat him special like any other companion.

We would spend New Years Eve at home once again as always while mom and Andreas went out with friends. Although I have not been able to sit down with mom and the rest of the family to reveal my secret, I fear I cannot avoid it to much longer. I see how she's pushing me into trying to have a relationship with Fernando but there are so many barriers and the inability to communicate is a humongous factor here. We watch the television specials and watch for the ball to drop on time square with Dick Clark It's nice that the girls will stay awake with me this year. I call Laddie over and rest on his back side anxiously waiting for the moment to happen.

CONSEQUENCES

The New Year 1979 arrives like any other with people driving through the neighborhood honking their horns screaming *Happy New Year* and firecrackers going off all over town. This is one of the most dangerous times of year to be outside and especially for your animals to be loose because of all the noise and the threat of irresponsible people shooting off firearms. They don't realize that the bullets they shoot in the air will inevitably come down somewhere. There is the highest potential for injury and death this day because of drunk drivers and others who over celebrate. So being home is where I am every New Years Eve.

I realize the consequences I will endure if I enter into another false hope relationship with Fernando so I'll just have to see what happens. Colleen has been seeing this guy from school named Manny and I think he's going to take her to her senior prom this year. I never attended my prom because I was up in Glendale but I would have liked to. That is one thing that happens only once in your lifetime and no matter who you are, senior prom is a milestone in your life and should not be missed under any circumstances if you can avoid it. I just added it to the list of regrets during my high school career along with the inability to produce a child.

The relationship mom was involved with was beginning to have some ugly spots in it of late. She has a new job and works in a factory in San Marcos off Mission and not far from my job. It isn't uncommon for her relationships with her boyfriends to turn physical as in the past and I hope she can restrain herself from doing him any harm. She is not a pleasant person when she's had too much to drink and more times then not ends up in a physical bout with her partners. However in her case it is the man who suffers the ultimate insult being beat up by a woman, an older woman at that even!

Like any abusive relationship I cannot comprehend why these younger guys stick around after the way she treats them. God, it is so embarrassing for me. I have changed jobs now and am back on first shift for the time being and know some of the girls in the department. I'm continuing with softball still but down to just one team now, the Breakers in Carlsbad. I caved into mom's persistence pleads to go out with Fernando. Why do I allow myself to be so weak when it comes to her? I discuss this in therapy but never bring up the most important reason why I'm there to begin with.

I'm going to be twenty one this year and want to find the courage to tell mom the truth. Michelle is doing okay in school but losing interest fast. Fernando takes me to a Spanish dance club in Santa Ana which only plays Mexican music. It's been a most difficult courtship because of the lack of understanding him. He gives me a box that comes more of a shock then a surprise. I haven't known him that long and already he wants to propose? The ring was petite with a solitary chip. I smiled because what else could I do? I do not care for diamonds and was at a loss for words.

I thought about this deeply and came to the only conclusion possible. I will marry this guy, move away from home and in a very short period of time get divorced. It is the only thing I can think of that will force me to deal with the reality I keep putting back in the closet. I call Lisa and ask her if she would be interested in being my maid of Honor. I had a lot of explaining to do but I knew she would understand. She has never been one to judge me and I respected and loved her for that. We would meet and go over the details. It was not something I was ready to announce to the entire family just yet but I needed some time to sort this out.

I would force myself to go along with this just once and although I know he will be hurt in the end, it's the price we both must pay. Lisa and I met shortly after asking her to be my maid of honor. It would be a small intimate service and just family and maybe very close friends like Christine Figueroa and Louise Pauu if I can find them. Lisa appeared to be in as much disbelief as I was but said nothing except; *are you sure you want to do this?* I did not have the heart to explain my motives so I told her yes, it's now or never! I told her I'd like Mrs. Kaahaaina to be my matron of honor and so we made arrangements to go over and visit her and her husband at home.

I felt badly deceiving them this way but these were extenuating circumstances and I was sure they would understand in the end. But for now I just don't have any more strength to fight either myself or mom over this fiasco. If this is what it takes for me to get out of this situation then it's what has to be done. I can only ask God's forgiveness and try to move on with my life. It's a very emotional situation and one I'm going to have to share with my therapist I fear. I don't tell anyone on my ball team either or at work. It's a private matter that I'll have no problem keeping to myself.

He insists moving in with me and I reluctantly agree. I won't invite him to any of my games for fear someone will find out. It will be a difficult situation to say the least having to sleep next to him at night. The girls seem unfazed with the situation and Andreas appears to be happy for him. There are plans to be made, a host of arrangements to consider yet I'm not at all prepared for all the things required for such an event in short notice. Lisa and I drive over to the Kaa-haaina's and give them the news. It is an uneasy and uncomfortable visit because it is painfully obvious I'm not sincere or the least bit excited like I should be.

I expressed how tired I was and that I was just nervous. She agreed to be my matron of honor and offered me her veil which she wore when she and David wed. I was so overcome with emotion that all I could do was tear up and thank her. This only compounded my inner grief because she is very sincere and it's a special offering meaning a great deal to her, to them. How can I possibly be so deceiving? By the end of the evening when we got up to leave, I thanked her both for agreeing to stand by me and the use of borrowing her veil. I was a wreck by the time I got home and Lisa questioned me again if I was sure about this.

I was desperate at this point and saw no other way out, it simply had to be done. In the preceding months of February and then March I struggled with the situation. I wasn't treating him kindly or in a loving manner and mom more then once asked me what was wrong. Apparently they have had conversations and he felt I wasn't ready because I wouldn't have sex with him. He would do his best to try but I always pretended to be asleep and refused to give in. I only became angrier with every attempt. I had already explained to mom very clearly and with the utmost conviction that we would under no circumstances engage in any sexual relations before we got married.

I don't know if mom told him this or not but before I agreed to let him move in with me and share my bed, I told her how I felt and that if he truly felt he loved me he would be able to concede to my wishes. I was not backing down or giving in and I was seriously adamant about it. In the meanwhile, I feel the stress of Matthew being in that hospital and mom going every week-end to visit him and how it was taking its toll on her. She had been drinking excessively when they went out dancing and would come home fighting already. It was most disturbing as well as embarrassing for me since the neighbors could here them carrying on.

One evening there was such a ruckus in her room that I went to see what they were carrying on about! Much to my disbelief mom had him pinned to the ground between the bed and her dresser and trying to hit him with a kitchen chair! My God, I thought; what is going on here and in the meanwhile she was yelling at him in Spanish and crying in the same breath. I called Colleen for assistance and to keep mom away from him. As I leaned over to protect and help him up mom swings the chair and hits me instead! Clearly that is the ultimate straw that breaks the camels back.

Only God knows what prevents me from striking my own mother. I get up in a rage and grab the chair which she is still gripping tightly and move it and her out of my way and storm out of the house. I get in my car and screech out of the driveway and drive off. I am livid by this point and have no idea where I'm going but continue driving. I could no longer cave in to her every whim just to please her. I have to take care of myself now and it is clear a decision has to be made. I drove towards San Diego where I would go to Aunt Rose's house. It's a Friday evening and the traffic is fairly light.

In my fits of rage in the past, I have gone to Glendale and stayed with Aunt Connie for the week-end trying to collect my thoughts. I could not, even back then, bring myself to tell her the honest truth about me. I didn't want to be responsible for causing her anymore pain she would endure by my sharing this information. Ordinarily it was times like this, emotional crisis that brought me to mutilate myself and take away the fit of anger which consumed me. The scars are everywhere on my body and although they are superficial they still bled and the pain went unfelt. I didn't feel guilty or ashamed for wanting to strike back at her but I honestly felt that if I had, someone would have died.

I'll never forget the incident between her and Kris when they got into and argument about something and he raised his hand to her, not so much as an attempt to strike her but to defend himself and she went ballistic. Dad had to grab hold of her and take her out in the backyard while Kris left the house. I don't remember what set her off but honest to God it left an indelible impression on me which nearly repeated tonight. Like her, I have absolutely no control over my temper when someone pushes me over the edge. She and I are done and I can safely say; *I am no longer your daughter, we are through!*

I can not be responsible for my actions around her and thus will remain away from the house for the rest of the evening and tomorrow. It all ends now and when I do go back I will tell Fernando that I cannot marry him. But not tell him why. I will call Lisa and the Kaahaaina's and tell them as well. I will further inquire of Lisa if I can come over and talk to her about something and finally tell her that I'm gay. I will tell Michelle as well and not concern myself with any negative responses. I cannot go on like this any longer. When I get to Aunt Rosemary's she can tell something is terribly wrong by the expression on my face.

I apologize to her for coming over so late and without calling first. She is a teacher and recognizes when someone is in distress which prompts her to ask me what's wrong. I told her the whole story about what went on tonight between mom and Andreas and how I was just trying to protect him and help him up. Then she proceeds to hit me on the back with the chair while I'm bent over assisting him! I was still livid over the entire situation and could speak no further. I fought back tears because I was so angry and she could tell I was distraught. She said she was going to call mom and let her know I was there.

I needed to be far away from mom, from her life as she lives it and away from her as a person. Her actions confirmed to me that I was less then insignificant to her and I meant nothing. It was what I had already known my whole life with her and the rest of the family since Grandma and Kristopher died. I didn't want to share any further family history about mom's behavior not just tonight but since dad left us. It wasn't worth the breath it would take me to tell her. Besides all that, she is her sister and I wasn't even sure she would believe me. I told her I was gay and that I hadn't told mom or anybody else up to now, she was the first.

I only shared that I've struggled all my life to figure out when and how to tell her but never found an appropriate time. She offered no words of wisdom or scripture recommendations as I had hoped but I was emotionally and mentally exhausted so the silence was just as well. I appreciated her listening to me if nothing else. She was gone nearly fifteen minutes while I sat and looked at the television she was watching. John was out with friends for the evening and I was sorry to have missed him once again. I had to question my own sanity and how I let it get this battered.

Depression came immediately afterwards and while I sat there waiting for her to return I made some life altering decisions. I came to the conclusion that I am not my mother's keeper and therefore it's not necessary for me to wait around for her approval or acceptance. My feelings for her are nonexistent at this moment and I can't recall if they ever existed to begin with. I am empathetic towards her on occasion but anything deeper is not there. It's sad to admit that we weren't even friends. It's seems the life long battle is over and nobody has won nor conceded. Walking away is the right thing to do while I still have an ounce of dignity left.

When she returned she said mom was on her way down and they would talk. I was too exhausted to even attempt to leave no matter hoe badly I wanted to. I felt paralyzed as she continued to talk and asked if I wanted a cup of tea or coffee. I would have rather had a shot of whiskey or bottle of wine but that wasn't going to happen! I didn't want to see her, look at her or even hear her voice. The rage had come from deep down and it was raging through my veins. Nothing good could possibly come from hearing anything she had to say. Naturally everything would be my fault and I had blown it all out of proportion.

I did not want another confrontation and can't even think of facing her again tonight. I didn't want to be sorry I drove down here for nothing. I needed an escape from her all my life and nothing I did enabled me to be free of her. There is no guilt here and the only feelings I have are now dormant. I felt like an old woman while I was sitting here waiting. I knew in my heart that this would not pass and my memory has been once again witness to the ever changing moods of my mother that I can bear no longer. She had arrived before the hour was up with Michelle and Colleen in tow.

I couldn't face her, didn't want to face her but then I was helpless to move so I remained where I was in the living room while they sat in the kitchen. The girls came into the room to watch television with me as well and give them some privacy. I refused to disrespect myself any longer and let the truth be known. I was prepared to die tonight just like I was once before and I had wished we would have gotten into it just to finish it. That rage and resentment has been building for a long time now and perhaps it's best hovering over us now so hopefully it won't recede and bury itself deep past the dungeon of my soul. We need a solution to the end here.

This incident is most definitely the next issue I will be discussing in therapy this coming week. I may not tell her I'm gay but I will share the events of the night. If my disposition does not change by then I could very well come right out and tell her my attraction towards other women. Hopefully that will prompt her to ask me to elaborate and then I will be forced to tell her. They sat in the kitchen it seems for hours before Aunt Rose called me in there. I didn't want to go, couldn't move at first then I stood up and went to face her. My head was pounding and my face was hot, I was warm all over.

I looked away when mom spoke. Didn't want to hear anything she said, not an apology, not an explanation, nothing! I just wanted away from her, out of the same room and as far away as I could get. I was done with her, done with the neglect, with the manipulation and intimidation. The resentment had come up full force and I was through, this was the end. We talked rather she talked, I sat. I didn't hear a word she said and when she raised her tone and told me to look at her I saw through her. I removed any trace amount of attachment there was from my senses, heart and soul.

I would not allow her to hurt me ever again. I could walk away and not look back nor feel either guilt or shame. I know what the Bible says about honor and respect of your parents but in the same breath, parents also need to earn their children's respect as well. At the conclusion of her conversation to me she insisted Michelle go home with me and she'd be leaving in a little bit after us. I guess she felt I wouldn't harm myself if I had someone in the car with me to protect me. I couldn't find anything to say on the drive home so we didn't talk but instead Michelle turned on the radio and sang to the music.

I was crying profusely inside but silent as ever on the outside. I would not let Michelle see me cry after a night such as tonight. She told me Fernando had packed his things and moved back to his boss's guest house. It was not a good way to start the New Year. Nothing more was ever brought up about that weekend and we moved around the house like total strangers mom and I. For Michelle's birthday we went to dinner and I was cordial but we barley spoke two sentences to one another. The girls I'm sure were uncomfortable but they better get used to it because until I move out this is how it is.

We went on about our lives as time moved along. Colleen was making her dress for the prom that Manuel promised to take her to. Mom had a new boyfriend who seemed to be a little more mature then Andreas. I would hear her cry some nights after coming home from dancing and all. I had been weakened by this entire chain of events and lost my way so to speak. I poured my heart out in therapy and left exhausted each time. There was no debate or suggestion of recourse and I couldn't deal with the massive amount of disappointed that had occurred. I needed some enlightenment but got none.

I called Lisa to see if I could see her and perhaps spend the night as I had a personal confession I wanted to share with her. It was important to me she be the first friend I tell. I was still uncertain when I would tell Mrs. Kaahaaina because I hadn't a clue what their religious beliefs were and I couldn't afford life without them. I had told Michelle that I was gay when we were in her room most recently and quite surprised at her response. She reacted as though she had a bad taste in her mouth and her forehead wrinkled up and cheeks puffed out! She didn't move away from me and I was glad about that but none the less she was uncertain exactly what that meant.

I went further by telling her it didn't mean anything or that I was going to change. I am still the same person, still the same sister and I didn't intend on bringing home any dates. I was not about to expose any woman to this house of uncertainty. She asked if mom knew and I told her I assumed Aunt Rose told her but that she's known all her life and she's been in denial of it ever since. She had lots of questions and I was happy to explain them to her. I explained to her how mom and I have always been at odds with one another from the very beginning it seems and how it progressively worsened downhill after each death starting with Grandma.

Lisa's reaction to the news was; *so what's the big deal?* I welcomed her whimsical response and was elated that she didn't react like Michelle did. She said she had her suspicions but first had to ask if I was sure it wasn't just a phase because I had such shitty luck with guys? I told her I was born this way but that I couldn't tell my parents, siblings or anybody because I didn't want to bring any shame or offend anyone in the family. I told her I never put too much into people's opinions of me because they didn't matter. I knew the only one that mattered was God. I was aware of what the bible says but I also know my Father, God. We have an understanding I told her.

I had an abrupt fling with this guy who was a friend of the family and unfortunately Colleen had caught us and was quite shocked by it. It was the last time I saw him and did anything at the house with anybody. Colleen was preparing to go to the prom this evening while mom was getting ready for her date with Raymond. This guy went to school with Clifford and we all knew his family since *Cerda* is a well known name around town. When the time had come for Manny to arrive and take her to dinner he was running late. She looked beautiful in her dress and hair all shinny and wavy. I was getting nervous and feeling bad that he might not show up.

Dinner time had come and gone and still no Manny. Raymond offered to take her but she insisted that something must have come up and she was going to change back into her pajamas and stay in her room. I felt so bad that I wanted to find this guy and see what was going on. Mom and Ray opted to stay home instead and had a few friends over to play cards and have a few beers. I was glad they stayed because I didn't know what Colleen must have been going through. It was a rude and cruel thing to do to someone and I hoped to God he had a more then perfect explanation like; a sudden death in the family!

Mom's birthday and mother's day would come and go with nothing spectacular going on. We all got together for dinner to celebrate the mothers but no special gift exchange was happening. I signed the card the girls bought her along with a box of candy but nothing else. Mom still goes to see Matthew on weekends as she's able and say's he's improving even if it's baby steps. His friend David has been to visit him as well. I didn't ask about dad because he really didn't matter. I had disowned both parents at this point and had no use for any information pertaining to them.

With graduation near I gave Colleen a crisp fifty dollar bill for her present and told her to have fun. She wasn't like me when it came to money. I was careless and spent it most of the time as soon as I accumulated it. Colleen on the other hand always had a plan for the funds she collected and worked for babysitting.

She was going to spend the summer in Los Angeles with our friends Luisa, Thwat and the two kids Renee and Boyd. They had kept in touch and Luisa asked her if she would be interested in coming up for the summer and care for the kids, they would send her the bus ticket.

It was good that she was getting away and graduation went well for her. I was glad she chose to stay at Oceanside High school where they would be graduation at the beach like I did three years ago. El Camino graduated on their football field. The beach was so much more meaningful then the landscape at El Camino. Of the two people I told I was gay, Colleen would be difficult to say those words to. We had had our differences in the past yet this was more personal and would effect our relationship differently I felt. I didn't know exactly how or what Colleen thought of me or felt about me.

I know she had an unbreakable relationship with mom and that she knew mom and I weren't in the best condition but that should make no difference. Colleen can be critical and speak before thinking things out so I had to choose my words carefully. I figured mom would have told her but apparently not. I changed softball teams when I met some girls from other teams and they invited me to join their team this summer, we played in Oceanside. I had had a great run with the Breakers and most of the girls remained on the team but I choose to move on. These girls I knew were gay like me and I wanted to be with my own people for once.

After graduation Colleen took the first bus out of town to go up North. She wasn't going to come home ever couple weeks like I use to. Colleen had a mind of her own and I was glad she took the initiative to do as she pleased no matter what. Michelle had a rough school year and was supposed to attend summer school which she did reluctantly. Mom and I had managed to talk every now and again and one night I had to sleep in her bed because I set off bombs in the garage to kill off the trillions of spiders that crawled around all night long. She said it was alright and it was rare that Raymond spent the night since he had his own home near by.

They seemed to be getting along fine without any confrontations or eruptions. This evening in particular after mom had come home, my cousin, her nephew Aunt Stella's youngest son Richard had come over wondering when Matthew was going to come back home. He had obviously been drinking as the stench of beer was on his breath and his clothes reeked with the same foul odor. Here mom and I are trying to get some sleep and he's trying to get into bed with us. We were both flabbergasted to say the least and mom had to tell him on more then once occasion to get out of here. She was his Aunt and I was his cousin what did he think he was doing?

He continued his persistence and insisted he wouldn't tell anybody! I was fearful he was going to say something about all those times he tried to molest me when I would go over and baby-sit his kids when he would stop back by the house because he forgot something. I felt so sorry for his wife Betty and his three kids, cute kids and he was so disgusting! I'm his cousin for God's sake and he's going to behave like this even in front of his Aunt! I wanted to shoot him! He kept persisting until mom threatened to call his mother right then! How absurd that he wouldn't stop until mom threatened to call his mother! What a sick bunch of boys they are!

First it was his brother Bill now he thinks he can just come into the room and take advantage? I so wanted to tell mom the story about Bill but we were past that anymore and I could share nothing of personal tragedy with her any longer. I couldn't even put it into words as I had once or twice in the past. I had my freedom from her finally but not entirely from myself. There was a woman at work who had been making passes at me for some time now. I ignored her because she was not only married but sleeping with some guy from work. I wasn't about to get involved in any more triangles again.

Although people at work constantly questioned me about my personal life and such I shared nothing. I didn't feel it was anybody's business that I was gay and therefore said nothing. There were a couple guys who asked me out but one in particular never gave up. Larry Berg seemed a big ball of fun and had asked me if I'd like to see a movie with him sometime not so much a date as rather just someone to see a movie with. I knew for a fact, everybody knew he was dating Judy from the lab and didn't want to intrude but he wasn't exclusive and that was fine with Judy.

I was to go back on nights for about six weeks as a rotation shift and that was alright with me too. Michelle was old enough to stay home by herself and mom didn't stay out that late since hooking up with Raymond. They did a lot of their drinking at the house because they played cards now, a new thing I guess. One week end I stayed home because we had a bye Teresa had come over to visit mom. I was doing some reading on the floor by the television and whatever mom and Teresa were talking about they kept trying to get a comment out of me. I wasn't really paying attention so I guess they thought I was blowing them off and Teresa wanted an answer.

She was a little agitated by this point and so dumped her glass of beer on my head while I was minding my own business reading. This got a reaction out of me instantaneously that even shocked myself that no sooner had I gotten to my feet and got hold of her so fast, picked her up and flung her to the ground landing on top of her so she couldn't move. I had no idea where that kind of strength came from but I had her restrained so quickly she didn't know what to do. Mom jumped up and demanded I let her up immediately if not sooner! I have never done anything like that before in my life and was shocked to be honest.

Sometimes you can never be fully aware or prepared for the consequences of everything that happens or everything that comes up. It happened so fast that I didn't know what to say once I helped her back up. She looked at me with equal amazement and quipped she was just fooling around with me. She assured me she wasn't mad just embarrassed and there was no need for me to apologize. I didn't realize I was so short tempered but I was aware that I had changed since that exchange between mom and me some months ago. I have yet to recover from that incident and perhaps I never will.

Some things in life cannot be mended no matter how much times passes. Some tragedies in life have no closure at all and all you can do is try your best to move on. There are no bridges to build between mom and I and that book is lost forever. Before the end of summer Colleen comes in the door one day with Renee and Boyd attached to either hand. I wait for Luisa and Thwat to come in directly behind her but nobody is there. I asked her what was going on and she said she drove down here with the kids because Luisa and Thwat had had a terrible fight and she feared for the kid's safety.

I asked her if she knew how to drive a stick shift and she said no, she learned by just getting in and driving down here, all the way from West Hollywood? That's a lot of freeway. I asked her if she realized they could call the police on her and charge her with kidnapping. She insisted with a stronger voice that they had a terrible fight and was afraid for the kids. Mom came in the room to find out what all the commotion was all about. She explained the situation once again to mom who in turn agreed with me by saying they had every right to call the police on her and charge her with kidnapping.

It didn't matter what the circumstances were, that didn't give her the right to steal not just their children but their car as well! All I could think of was this girls got balls! The kids were fine and just wanted something to eat so I went to Burger King like they asked and bought them some food. Mom would call Luisa and talk to her hoping she wouldn't call the police. By the time I returned mom said she talked with Luisa and that they were on their way down and that they were not going to call the police. I don't know how mom convinced them not to involve the authorities but Colleen is awful lucky. Kidnapping and grand theft is a very serious crime!

That didn't seem to faze her in the least because all she could think about were the children and their welfare. I suppose that's a commendable character trait but none the less, wow! I have to admire the girl, she's got no scruples. By the end of the week-end things had been reconciled between Luisa, Thwat and Colleen. The kids were in no danger they assured Colleen and they made it clear she would be invited back once again if she so chose. They had brought the rest of her things down which she left behind and wanted to be sure she understood there were no hard feelings. They understood her motive and it wasn't like to happen again.

I'm sure the kids hadn't a clue what had happened they were just excited to come down and visit me. They had grown very fond of Colleen; she had that effect on some people's children. I didn't want her to think I was picking on her but I had to throw my last two cents in about the entire situation. What she did was very brave on all counts but she put those kids in more danger then their parents. What would have happened if she got into an accident and one of those kids was seriously hurt or killed? She would spend the rest of her life in jail under the circumstances.

I wanted her to be completely aware of the consequences she's dealing with when she takes matters into her own hands. No matter what went on in their house, her actions were inexcusable and irresponsible. Mom was less critical but those two had their own language that only they spoke therefore I suppose mom took care of the situation with her and it wasn't likely to happen again. Perhaps she will think twice about situations like that if it happens again or any situation for that matter. I had agreed to go to the movies on more then one occasion with Larry and his daughter Wendy.

He was a nice guy, laughed a lot and his daughter was very cute. His next adventure was a trip to Anaheim for the ski show they had annually and although I didn't ski I went along just for the hell of it. He seemed to be very entertaining and it was a welcome change for a guy not wanting to get into my pants. I would have no problem however telling them I was gay if it came to that. I've come to realize that there is no shame in being gay and if people are offended, it's their problem not mine. I will always remember the summer of 79 being the year I changed my life. The door has been unlocked and it's up to me to walk out it.

I had given in one last time to a friend of mine who owned the gas station by the high school. I felt oddly obligated to date him for having taken such good care of my care when I was in dire straits and could not afford all the repairs. What I did learn from him was the intricate workings of an engine which he tried on several occasions to teach me how to repair on my own. I would purchase the parts and he would teach me how to install them. He was more a mentor then a lover and I was tormented by how and what I felt towards him. He was very kind and giving. I felt I should show him kindness in reply.

He wanted more of me then I could possibly offer. Our sexual rendezvous left me depressed and emotionally paralyzed. I could not continue this affair any further and when his daughter came out from Colorado for a visit she asked me; are you a lesbian? I couldn't catch my breath for a moment and asked why she would ask such a question? She said because it was something her father had mentioned in one of their discussions. Gerry had tried on many occasions to show me how to manage my money so I wouldn't be dependent on anyone but myself. I didn't know if I could trust him with my five hundred dollar savings and kept putting him off.

He never pressured me to do anything but kept insisting that women should always look to be self sufficient and not dependent on a man for anything. I would respond that men were not a problem for me. The intimacy between us was not genuine or sincere and somehow he knew that. He was old enough to be my father and I suppose at that age they know these things about women. I knew one of his other lady friends and he told me how he'd been helping her buy and sell real estate so she could establish her own money and live self sufficiently. I wanted to do that but not willing to be intimate or obligated to him for it.

I owed him for his kindness in a big way but not how he wanted. I was young and impressionable but I have my own battles to concur and he would just be complicating my situation further. By the end of summer I had broken off our affair and apologized profusely. I can see where he would be the best person for me in means of establishing financial security and well being but there was one big disadvantage, he was a man. I was still uncertain of any future at all and therefore could not see that far into it. I choose to live one day at a time. My needs were that of another woman and unless or until I could fulfill those wishes, I was insignificant even to myself.

I had swallowed my pride where mom was concerned and on Fridays would take her flowers and lunch at work. I liked knowing that she was probably the only woman who for the time being was getting flowers every Friday and lunch brought to her by her three daughters. I'm certain that she didn't brag about her three daughters and sons or share any personal information about us as well but the point was, she is the only mother we'll ever have and no matter what our shortcomings our family is what it is, stuck together with a bit of hope and prayer there may be a chance for us after all.

It was not long after this when Michelle had returned back to school and Colleen was doing her thing that I had brought Gloria over on occasion to meet the girls and mom and sit around to watch television. Our visits were always brief but I needed them to be aware of whom I truly was. She was not my girlfriend or a companion but a friend. There were glances of uneasiness and odd stares at first but after a few visits they had an idea of what direction this was all headed. I was no longer willing to remain hidden behind a closet with a glass door.

Gloria was older and mom didn't seem too happy about that but she understood we were just friends.

The time was near that I was about to move on in my life and mom and the girls would have to accept that like it or not. Therapy would continue as I would attempt to share my truth with her as well, the whole ugly truth from the beginning. It would be more tortuous an issue to confront then the gay issue but in order for me to even think about healing I would have to expose the root of the wound face on. I realize that it isn't about being gay but more so how insignificant I feel because of being seen as that and only that. My long battles with depression and suicide were still far from over but maybe now I can share why they exist.

Society is far from understanding homosexuality and as long as they are blinded by fear and ignorance our struggles for acceptance will continue and remain unresolved. I choose to take a higher road in educating my family and friends. To enlighten them to the truth of whom we are and what we are. This isn't just a new beginning for them as much as it is for me as well. I have just as much to learn in the process as them. God willing, all will turn out for the best for all of us.

978-0-595-42065-
0-595-42065-6

Printed in the United Kingdom
by Lightning Source UK Ltd.
118824UK00001B/283